LOVE,
THE **DRUG**

From the Trap of Addiction
to the Freedom of Recovery

PAIGE ABBOTT
RAJU HAJELA
SUE NEWTON

 Friesenpress

Suite 300 - 990 Fort St
Victoria, BC, V8V 3K2
Canada

www.friesenpress.com

ISBN
978-1-5255-5808-5 (Hardcover)
978-1-5255-5809-2 (Paperback)
978-1-5255-5810-8 (eBook)

1. Self-help, Codependency

Distributed to the trade by The Ingram Book Company

Table of Contents

Acknowledgements

Thank you to all our clients and patients who have been willing to look at relationships in their recovery from Addiction. What the disease of Addiction looks like in this area and how recovery is possible requires steadfast exploration with honesty and humility.

We dedicate this book to the billions of people worldwide who have been personally affected by Addiction involving relationships and those who are connected to those affected by the disease, which is all of us!

Introduction

Everyone has relationships at three fundamental levels – with self, with others, and with whatever concept of the universe or creation one may have, which can be referred to as spirituality. There can be problems inherent in those relationships because of beliefs, values, perceptions, expectations, and wanting things to happen a certain way. Sometimes there is a great deal of preoccupation with being the best or making the relationship the best in accord with some standard, whether it be personal, cultural, or set by principles and scriptures of a religion to which one feels connected.

The disease of Addiction that is often associated with substances, is fundamentally rooted in relationships. Addiction affects how one interacts with self, others, and spirituality. It impacts perception, values, beliefs, behaviours, and feelings. The level of relationships can be an uncomfortable one for people to explore in recovery. This exploration requires individuals to expand their awareness, examine their beliefs, and look honestly at things that the disease wants to avoid. The idea that some of these beliefs may be fantasies that have been created over many years and used by the disease can be difficult to fathom. However, for recovery growth to occur, challenging the underlying beliefs and values is essential and builds the foundation for health and recovery. It is a process to move towards optimal health and one that requires addressing the problems that may exist at all three levels of relationships.

This book is intended for those who have the disease of Addiction and those who are in relationships with those with Addiction. The disease of Addiction is so common around the world that every human being on this planet either has the disease or knows someone quite personally with this disease, such as a relative, friend, colleague, or client. As we have discussed in the book *Addiction is Addiction* (Hajela, Newton, Abbott, 2015), everyone can benefit from incorporating recovery into their life. This book outlines the signs and symptoms of the disease in the realm of relationships, as well as recovery principles. We have used male and female names for ease of illustration. We have tried to incorporate various types of relationship examples. We hope our readers will recognize that the ideas apply and are translatable to all types of relationships – family, friends, lovers – of any gender identification or combination.

Definition of Addiction
Involving Relationships

Addiction is a primary, chronic disease of brain reward, motivation, memory, and related circuitry. Dysfunction in these circuits leads to characteristic biological, psychological, social, and spiritual manifestations. This is reflected in an individual pathologically pursuing reward and/or relief with substance use and other behaviours. Although problematic substance use is often associated with Addiction, the disease in the brain impacts many aspects of the person, including behaviour, thinking, feeling, and relationships. Addiction involving relationships is an aspect that everyone with the disease is vulnerable to. It can involve enmeshment, avoidance, isolation, craving, poor communication, abusiveness, control, manipulation, anorexia, and/or bingeing, intermixed with periods of health.

> Addiction involving relationships
> is an aspect that everyone with the disease is
> vulnerable to.

Although some people use the term 'co-dependency' when referring to Addiction involving relationships, we emphasize that, practically, 'co-dependency' refers to a problem that involves preoccupation with a relationship that may or may not have Addiction in it. 'Co-dependency' in terms of relationships can be likened to hazardous or harmful substance use that occurs in the absence of Addiction. With awareness and education, the symptoms can remit indefinitely. The disease of Addiction is a more serious, primary, chronic brain disease that impacts all aspects of health. The chronicity of Addiction is characterized by periods of relapse and remission, which can be aggravated in its myriad forms, especially if Addiction involving relationships is not addressed. These relapses will occur in some form despite awareness, education, and ongoing recovery work, as Addiction is a chronic condition with no cure. Recovery from Addiction involving relationships involves addressing bio-psycho-social-spiritual health with a focus on boundaries, communication, detachment, and interdependence.

The description of Addiction above is part of the definition of Addiction promulgated by the American Society of Addiction Medicine (ASAM, 2011). Addiction is further characterized by:

A. Inability to consistently abstain

B. Impairment in behavioural control

C. Craving

D. Diminished recognition of significant problems in one's behaviour and interpersonal relationships

E. A dysfunctional emotional response

Addiction involving relationships with or without problematic substance use fits the ABCDE. The A, B, C can be active with substances as well as behaviours, including relationships, and are typically less active during periods of remission, particularly cravings. The D happens because of conscious or sub-conscious avoidance, which people often call denial. The E is often experienced as a blunted or non-reaction to an issue that is emotionally charged (e.g., a loved one's death or physical abuse) or an over the top emotional outburst to an issue that is minor in the whole scheme of things (e.g., dishes being left in the sink or someone forgetting about a commitment).

ASAM has developed a definition of abstinence to be, "intentional and consistent restraint from the pathological pursuit of reward and/or relief that involves the use of substances and other behaviours. These behaviours may involve, but are not necessarily limited to, gambling, video gaming, spending, compulsive eating, compulsive exercise, or compulsive sexual behaviours." (ASAM, 2013). Thus abstinence, in the behavioural context, can be defined as an individual establishing restraint to a level determined by the individual, in consultation with their treatment provider and peer support circle. Regarding psychoactive substances, no use is considered ideal. However, in the spirit of harm reduction, the principle of restraint may be utilized to engage in recovery from Addiction involving any or all aspects of the disease.

Part I:
The Disease

Chapter 1: Addiction

"No one would have identified me as having Addiction. I didn't do drugs, barely touched alcohol, and seemed to be balanced in my life. They were wrong. My name is Jolene, and I am a person with Addiction. I grew up in a happy enough home with a mother, father, and younger brother. I remember being teased by my family at a young age for being a daydreamer. I loved creating stories in my mind and imagining I was in a different place, time, and reality. I was a bit of a loner at school, though I had some friends. I didn't have my first boyfriend until I was 19. I remember we fought a lot because I was jealous and insecure, always thinking he was going to leave me for someone better. I ended the relationship when I was 21, as I was too scared. Scared he would leave me or hurt me or figure out I wasn't that great after all. After that, I dated around for years, sometimes faithful to my partner, sometimes not. I met Rich, my current husband, when I was 30, and it was love at first sight. We moved in together within six months and then started talking marriage and family. I never knew I wanted these things before, but suddenly, I could think of nothing but. We had three children before I turned 35. I lived for those kids, and now they are older and don't need me as much. I find myself feeling lonely and in angst much of the time. What do I do with my time? Who am I?

I am Jolene, and people are my drug."

Jolene is one example of many who struggle with Addiction involving relationships. Many people can identify as having Addiction involving substances (or being "addicted to" something, as the common vernacular goes). Yet these same people may be unable to see how Addiction impacts other parts of their lives and behaviours, including relationships with others. These issues in relationships may be directly related to substance use (e.g., people being mad because of ongoing drug use or detaching because of how people act when intoxicated), but this is not always the case. The symptoms that Jolene describes, including fantasy from a young age, shame, insecurity, sexual promiscuity, and enmeshment, are common features of Addiction involving relationships that occur with or without substance use. As in Jolene's case, substances were barely part of the picture for her, yet issues with relationships and fantasy were there from a young age and blossomed over time. In the coming chapters of this book, we review the common features of Addiction involving relationships and elements of recovery.

WHAT IS ADDICTION?

Addiction is a disease of the brain. It is created primarily by genetics, which then interact with the environment and other vulnerabilities, including stress, exposure to substances, behaviours, and trauma. Addiction affects brain function, so in addition to behaviour, it impacts how people think, perceive the world, deal with feelings, connect to others, and have a spiritual relationship. Many people are vulnerable to Addiction, meaning that they carry some genetic predisposition. This does not mean that the disease will always manifest; however, the more exposure there is to substances, dysfunctional environment(s), relationship(s), and stress, the more likely people are to manifest the disease and experience serious complications from it.

Addiction is a chronic, lifelong disease. This means that, without proper treatment, there is progression in symptoms. Addiction can present as mild, moderate, or severe, and this varies depending on the individual, with no rhyme or reason why one person manifests mild symptoms while others may have severe symptoms by their teenage years. As with other diseases, manifestation and progression is variable, but there are common key features of the disease amongst people. This book is based on the key symptoms that we have observed in practice with individuals who have Addiction involving relationships. As you read through the book, we encourage you to look for the similarities (what you can relate to), keeping in mind that your brain will be on the hunt for differences (what you do not identify with), to further isolate you in your addictive thinking and prevent recovery engagement.

> Addiction is a chronic,
> lifelong disease.

ADDICTION BEYOND SUBSTANCES

In Jolene's story, escape involving fantasy (and likely other features of Addiction, as well) was present from a young age. This then progressed into other symptoms of Addiction involving relationships. Relationships, as well as food and technology (e.g., video games, smartphones, television) are the most common ways that Addiction manifests before any exposure to drugs or alcohol occurs. There is further risk when drugs, alcohol, sex, and other behaviours, including things like gambling or even work or exercise, are introduced to the young person and they begin to engage. Without knowing they are at risk for Addiction, a strong attachment to these behaviours can develop and unwittingly exacerbate the disease and fuel progression.

Our hope in writing this book is to promote awareness for everyone so that you can be more aware of family history and consider environment, exposure, and stress that is happening in your life that could activate or exacerbate underlying vulnerabilities.

A family history of Addiction may be trickier to identify when one moves outside of the realms of drugs and alcohol. Issues with relationships, but also other behaviours like food and work, are so misunderstood, undervalued, and often not placed in the Addiction category that people deny they have a family history. There is no need to go around diagnosing family members as having Addiction or not. Rather, it is important to appreciate that there is likely some degree of vulnerability for Addiction, whether that is obvious or not, as Addiction exists in all genetic pools around the world. Therefore, appreciating that there is some degree of risk and being more open and honest about the places being frequented (internally and externally), the substances and behaviours engaged with, and levels of stress and ability to cope with feelings will help with overall health and well-being.

Those who identify having Addiction involving substances

benefit from pursuing abstinence from these psychoactive substances. However, recovery requires much more than abstinence. Exploring the topics in this book related to Addiction involving relationships is an essential part of recovery.

Those who identify having Addiction involving relationships will benefit from pursuing boundaries and exploring the topics of each chapter of this book. It is also important to abstain from mood-altering substances, including alcohol, nicotine, marijuana, other drugs, certain prescription medications, and preferably, caffeine. Sugar is increasingly being recognized as a problem as well, so exploring restraint there becomes important too. In other words, those who have Addiction are vulnerable to having the 'disease of more' pervade all areas of their life. Addiction leaves no area untouched. As Addiction resides in the brain, it impacts all levels of self and behaviour in varying proportions and degrees, depending on the level of disease activity at the time.

Those who do not identify having Addiction of any sort would also benefit from pursuing boundaries and would be encouraged to consider pursuing restraint from the substances listed above, as none of these are needed for health.

Addiction is a disease of escape, reward, and/or relief. The brain pursues these in a way that becomes dysfunctional. Initially there may be escape, reward, and/or relief, but over time it may feel awful and/or become destructive to health and well-being. The pursuit of escape, reward, and relief trumps anything else and people find themselves obsessing and engaging in behaviours that they do not want to engage in at the expense of other parts of life.

Throughout this book, we emphasize the need for continued openness and willingness to explore relationships with others, self, and spirituality to continue unfolding the journey of health and recovery.

Chapter 2: Intoxication

Amy was excited to have met Brad at the party her friends invited her to. She had gone reluctantly, as she was still obsessing over losing Art, who she had been with for five years. Art was so good looking and successful in his business. He had showered Amy with presents and attention and provided her with lots of money and life comforts. He was very busy with work and pursuing new opportunities to get ahead. He liked the idea of being a father, although he did not appear to know what that meant. He had lost his father early in his life and worked hard to get established. Amy thought that she could make up for it all by being the best mother to their children. She got pregnant without really discussing it with Art, as she was certain that a lifetime with Art was what was 'meant to be', especially since he was so affectionate and demonstrative of his love for her. Art got busier at work when Amy was pregnant and was hardly available emotionally or physically when Jason was born. Amy was happy to be a mother. However, it was hard as she felt like a single mother. Art was angry and yelled a lot whenever he was home, especially if Jason needed some attention or Amy was not able to meet Art's needs. Amy also could not overlook Art's constant flirting with other women and ignore the stories that she heard about other women in Art's life. She didn't ask questions because she loved Art unconditionally and trusted him. He liked porn like all men she knew, and she hoped he would satisfy his urges that way rather than with other women.

Sadly, the 'fairy tale' ended when Art announced that he wanted to be with someone else rather than Amy and Jason. It was a devastating blow, as Amy had been ready to do anything that Art wanted. She was even okay with occasional affairs if Art would marry her, which would clarify status and a wonderful lifestyle for Amy and Jason. Even though she wanted more children, she had come to accept that Art didn't, so she was going to be happy with Jason. She tried hard to convince him to get married, but he was hesitant; and now he was gone.

Amy never thought she would love anyone else again, yet it had only been two months and she had just met Brad. Jessica said that she had known him for about six months through her work and felt that he was perfect for Amy. Brad was so attentive to Amy at the party; it felt like the party was just for her. He made Amy forget all her troubles with Art. He was a single dad. He told her that his wife cheated on him, so he had left about a year ago. He loved his daughter, Crystal, who was now three years old. He had dreams of having a large family, just like Amy. He had already planned a week away in Mexico together, if she agreed to go out with him. It felt so magical and so right.

People are generally familiar with the euphoria that is produced by substances, especially alcohol or opioids. It is a feeling of not caring about any problems they may have been experiencing. As much as people desire it, it is chemically induced and persists for the duration of effect of the substance on the brain, including the release of dopamine in the reward circuitry.

INTOXICATION IN RELATIONSHIPS

Intoxication in relationships is much longer lasting and is mediated by natural chemicals in the brain, which include dopamine and glutamate. People can easily relate to the feeling of 'falling in love', which is idealized in our society, which really is intoxication. People can call it 'chemistry' or 'attraction', but it has an element of fantasy attached to it, as that impulse of 'falling in love' is usually based on little information about the person (object of desire). The natural chemicals produced in the brain in response to that feeling create a euphoria, not caring about any problems in the world and/or feeling that the problems one has will be (re)solved in the company of the person.

This intoxication can be a roller-coaster ride as the fantasy turns to obsession in the form of wanting to know how the other person feels, second guessing what they may or may not say, extrapolating meaning from what they have or have not said. Even the sorrow can be romanticized, sometimes in the presence of physical or emotional abuse. The Kenny Rogers song *I Wish I Could Hurt That Way Again* expresses this well – "I wish I could hurt that way again, at least I had you every now and then, and in between the sorrows, at least there was tomorrow, and as long as there's tomorrow, there's no need . . ."

> Intoxication can be a roller-coaster ride as the fantasy turns to obsession.

Intoxication in relationships is a form of getting attention that feels good and/or brings relief from any negativity a person may be feeling. Intoxication can also come from being the object of desire for someone else, even in the absence of any personal attraction on your part with that person. 'Wanting to be wanted' is the impulse that is satisfied with feeling wanted or feeling needed, which is a reward, regardless of what the reality of the relationship may or may not be.

In Amy's story, the reader can hopefully connect with intoxication keeping Amy with Art initially, even though it was framed as 'love' or 'commitment'. Ending intoxication with a breakup or even the threat of a breakup precipitates withdrawal. Amy experienced this but then found Brad, with whom she appears to be back in intoxication. More discussion about withdrawal will come in the 'Recovery' section.

FEELINGS AND INTOXICATION

It is also important to appreciate that feelings in relationships, such as shame, anger, resentment and fear, can be part of intoxication (along with withdrawal and enmeshment) with Addiction involving relationships. Our brains receive a dopamine hit in the presence of strong feeling states, so these can be used to precipitate intoxication and can feed into withdrawal if intensity is not continued to be matched. Enmeshment comes when the individual is chasing intoxication, whether from intense feeling states or other behaviour. If Amy had not become intoxicated with Brad so quickly after the breakup with Art, she may have experienced prolonged withdrawal and/or intoxication with her feelings that would act as a barrier to moving forward in her life with a clearer vision of who she is, rather than being attached to a fantasy of what life 'should be'.

Chapter 3: Enmeshment

WHAT IS ENMESHMENT?

When someone is in a relationship for many years, enmeshment happens naturally. Enmeshment occurs because people are part of each other's lives and doing for each other, accommodating the other, or compromising becomes a way of life. Enmeshment, by its very nature, means becoming part of a web rather than being able to maintain one's identity. It starts with attachment at conception. Whether a child is wanted or not, the pregnancy itself creates a connection for the mother and father that is not only biological but emotional. People who have no biological connection, adoptive parents, for example, establish an emotional connection or attachment, too.

With attachment over a long period of time, people start to feel that they are part of each other's lives. Depending on the degree of closeness, together with desire and opportunity to spend time together, their lives become intertwined. This can become such that each person has difficulties in making decisions for oneself without considering the other's needs or putting the needs of another before one's own. This becomes especially significant if there is any perception that one can meet the needs of another that they may not be able to meet for themselves, by themselves. This is the reason enmeshment can happen in professional relationships as well as with colleagues, client relationships, or doctor-patient relationships where there is a perceived need that another can address or satisfy.

THE IMPACT OF ENMESHMENT

Enmeshment in one situation usually leads to more complications, rather than being limited to that situation alone, resulting in a lot of confusion, hurt, anger, frustration, and inability to act to step away from dysfunction. An example of this is in Joe's story.

Joe and his brother, Moe, were very close growing up. Joe remembers being an only child and wanting a brother. It finally happened around his ninth birthday. Moe was so cute and fun, even when Joe was in his teens. His girlfriends from the very beginning liked Moe. Joe thought having Moe around gave him an "in" with girls who he thought would make good mothers for his children. Joe also shielded Moe from their parents, as Dad was an alcoholic and Mom was always trying to cover up for Dad. Moe ran away from home when he was 15 and came to live with Joe, as Joe was trying to get established in life as a trucker. He and Anne had been living together for a few years and had a baby boy, Kyle. Although it was a financial and emotional strain to have Moe come and live with them, Joe could not turn his back on his brother, who Anne also felt close to. Soon thereafter, Joe and Anne had a baby girl, Dee. They had very little but made do with what they had. However, Moe got into heavy drinking and drugs. Anne became more preoccupied with the children. Joe felt more and more disconnected. By the time he was in his early 30s, he felt overburdened by the demands of work and family. He was annoyed by Anne buying things for the kids and spending money when he was away. He was also having to rescue Moe constantly as he got into more and more trouble with not being able to hold a job, getting in legal difficulties with car accidents and DUIs. Joe wanted to include him in playing hockey, which he enjoyed when they were younger, but now he was only interested in drinking, darts, and videogames. Joe didn't know where to turn.

Joe consulted his doctor about the stresses in his life. The doctor was very sympathetic and gave him some medication to help him relax and get a good night's sleep, which was challenging with all the problems that Joe had to deal with daily. The Xanax was very quick acting and made Joe calm when people were making demands of him. He needed more and more medication to feel this way, as anxiety started to build up over time. Joe and Anne fought a lot over the kids and about Moe. It reached a point where the doctor said Xanax was not good for him to take regularly and transitioned Joe to clonazepam.

Joe used to be a hockey player in his teens, and the doctor encouraged him to get some outlets for himself. So, he decided to play hockey again with his buddies when he could, and he also got involved in coaching hockey, as his son, Kyle, started to play hockey, too. Kyle became best friends with Jim, whose dad was an alcoholic and had abandoned the family, leaving Jim's mother, Fran, to raise him by herself. Joe got really close to Jim and Fran. He was getting increasingly more confused about what to do with Anne, as he and Fran were now involved sexually.

As is evident in Joe's story, his enmeshment issues go back a long time – to his childhood. There is a clear connection with the family history of Addiction. Joe has had difficulties connecting with what he needs to do to live his own life rather than rescuing and enabling other people. Although he means well, taking care of people he loves, he has interfered with the process of them being and becoming their own people. It started with Moe but progressed on to Anne and now Fran. His children and Jim get hurt as bystanders, yet would have their own issues to deal with, just as Moe, Anne, and Fran have. Their enmeshment with Joe, and Joe's enmeshment with them, underscores what a web of confusion enmeshment can become, with people feeling trapped and paralyzed, seemingly unable to figure out what the healthy actions would be.

The dilemmas Joe faces centre around how to best help himself while supporting (not enabling) the people in his life that he cares about. This includes what to do about the situation with Fran and Jim, as well as with his own nuclear family and family of origin, particularly Moe.

Joe's story demonstrates enmeshment with family of origin, chosen family, and how that can extend to other relationships, which then get confused as to their purpose and intent. Is he in love with Fran, or is it an escape from the pain of his own life? Fantasy plays a huge role in this as well, as Joe has seemed to carry an idyllic image of family from a young age when he wanted a sibling. This fantasy has carried through into his own family and now this new relationship with Fran and Jim.

Enmeshment is when the brain gets tied to ideas of what should be and how we want life to look, which can lead to control. It can also be linked to people-pleasing and caretaking, where again, the brain has an image of how things should

look and goes out of its way to try and promote this outcome
without rocking the boat, which can lead to enabling.

> Enmeshment is when the brain
> gets tied to ideas of what should be
> and how we want life to look,
> which can lead to control.

Chapter 4: Enabling

"Watching my daughter struggle with Addiction involving alcohol has been the most painful thing for me to endure. Hearing her come home at night intoxicated, stumbling around, is difficult. I'm more comfortable when she is home, and I'm distressed when she is out and I have no idea where she is or what she's doing. Is she okay? I have no idea. I will call and text her, usually with no response. What is my responsibility as a mother? As a person? I cannot just let this individual fall. I was convinced I could help. I found a local treatment facility, called them to schedule an appointment, took my daughter there. She bounced out of there quickly; it wasn't the help she needed at the time, I guess. I helped her with school, then later to find a job and work. She kept getting terminated and going through periods of unemployment, so I found my daughter a job at my company. That way, I could put in a good word with management if things went sideways. If she is working, there is some stability there. We don't talk much, although she does want to open up when she's been drinking, and I'm happy to listen. We have great conversations then, and I provide her with solutions, strategies, and comfort. Regrettably, nothing changes the next day, and she shuts me out. I will keep trying; why would I not? I am a compassionate person, and I care about my daughter."

—Anita

Enabling, by definition, is to give someone the authority and means to do something. Addiction involving relationships takes this and twists it around, such that enabling becomes lying, covering up, rescuing, and is a disempowering process where selfish gain is disguised as helping. Saving a loved one from acute pain and turmoil feels more comfortable than watching them be hurt. Ironically, in this act of 'preventing' hurt, there is tremendous hurt happening. Enabling robs all the opportunity for awareness, growth, and being able to say, "I did this myself." The enabler also becomes disconnected from his/her own feelings, not recognizing that the rescuing is a process of avoiding dealing with one's own powerlessness over the behaviour of a loved one.

THE ENABLER

The enabler often finds themselves self-acting, which may involve tasks, projects, busywork, and even other people's pain, to keep life looking smooth and together. The enabler may like being viewed as the hero or martyr who is there to support others, no matter what. There is a lot of image management in enabling. The person who is enabling does not really want the dysfunction to continue, so they do their best to 'fix' it, but all they are doing is putting a Band-Aid on a gaping wound.

Anita's story is just one example of how helping her daughter with school, getting a job, and treatment has the illusion of being helpful, but how motivated will Anita's daughter be to do these things for herself if they are being done for her? What would happen if Anita stopped these behaviours? This last question fuels a great deal of fear for people with Addiction involving relationships. Anticipated disaster and death are seemingly the only possibilities if one were to let go of enabling, which is framed as helping and support. Certainly, these are possibilities when Addiction is involved, but it is important to remember these are possible *even if* someone continues to be there to rescue. There is no guarantee that Anita's daughter will be safe as things stand currently. Rescuing can inadvertently promote the outcome that a person fears the most as it prevents them from seeing the full extent of their issues. Since Anita's daughter is having life staples provided for her, she is less likely to re-evaluate her life and take steps towards change, while driving the disease further. Therefore, rescuing enables the dysfunction rather than supports the solution, which is recovery. Recovery involves accountability, responsibility, and action. Enabling takes away the need for these as it provides an artificial safety net.

> Rescuing enables the dysfunction rather than supports the solution, which is recovery.

AVOIDANCE IS NOT A SOLUTION

People struggling with enabling behaviour may be so consumed by fear that they turn to avoidance for comfort. They may be engaged in action that is to rescue, or they may be pretending that everything is okay, even when it is clearly not. This allows the disease to continue to flourish because there is no accountability or need for change. It is important to remember, here, that enabling can be a symptom of Addiction involving relationships. Therefore, it is not only the person who is being enabled that has the disease, but the person engaged in the enabling behaviour, too. It can be easy to hide, as the enabler, behind a veneer of "they are sicker than me," or, "they are the sick one; I'm not." It takes honesty and courage to acknowledge these are unhealthy behaviours.

WHAT FEEDS ENABLING

Fundamentally, those with Addiction involving relationships have great discomfort sitting with pain in self and others. Strategies to minimize this pain in self and others are used, such as: rescuing, avoidance, enabling, control, and image management to name a few. These behaviours only serve to perpetuate the problem – and the pain – in the long-term. Short-term, they may provide temporary relief from the pain, which is alluring, but ultimately, they do not actually address anything. By Anita providing schooling and work for her daughter, this gives a false sense of security, reassurance, and comfort that everything is okay. As a result, Anita is more likely to keep engaging in these behaviours moving forward, and her daughter's drinking and other Addiction symptoms are likely to continue and get worse. Even arranging treatment, which many would say is helpful, enables the dysfunction to continue, because even if her daughter does attend the program, her motivation will be to appease and tell everyone what they want to hear, rather than being real.

> Those with Addiction have
> great discomfort sitting with
> pain in self and others.

ENABLING PROVIDES TEMPORARY RELIEF

The 12-Step programs talk about people hitting 'rock bottom' in order to change. This does not necessarily mean joblessness, homelessness, near death, or complete devastation in one's life for awareness to build that something needs to change. It can happen whenever the individual says, "Enough, I am now going to take some responsibility for my life." Enabling (covering up the problems or avoiding them altogether) delays this process, and in the meantime, Addiction is progressive, so symptoms will worsen over time. When the person who is being enabled finally comes to recognize there is an issue, things may be more severe and, therefore, harder to change than if they were not being enabled and less time had progressed.

Enabling provides temporary relief and comfort, but it enables the disease, not recovery. There are also a lot of expectations involved with enabling, which is the topic of the next chapter.

Chapter 5: Expectations

Sally was excited to see Paul in a few days, as he had been away for work for the past two weeks, and she really missed him. Even though they had talked regularly while he was away, she was eager to spend quality time together and wanted to surprise him with a fabulous meal. Over the next two days, Sally spent time figuring out what to cook, getting groceries, and tidying up the apartment, as she knew he would appreciate that. When it came time to pick Paul up from the airport, she made sure to get there ahead of time and was waiting for him when he came out. When she caught a glimpse of Paul, she broke out into a smile, running towards him to give him a big hug and kiss. Paul appeared distracted when she hugged him, and it felt as though he only gave her a half-hearted hug and kiss. Sally pulled away, asking Paul if he was okay. He didn't say much other than he was tired and stressed, as it had been a busy two weeks. Paul was quiet on the way home in the car, so Sally chatted happily to him. She told him about the surprise dinner she had planned to welcome him home. Once home, Sally continued to get the meal finished while Paul unpacked. She told him she would let him know when dinner was ready. With the candles lit, the table set, and dinner ready, Sally went into the bedroom to let Paul know. To her disappointment, she found him asleep on the bed with his suitcase still packed. She couldn't believe how angry she became that Paul would do this to her after she had gone to so much effort. Didn't he realize how much work she had put into this for him? She stormed out of the bedroom, blew the candles out, left the meal on the counter, grabbed her keys, and drove away. If he wasn't going to try to have dinner with her, why should she be there when he woke up?

Expectations are the strong belief that something should happen. They may or may not be realistic. Expectations are rigid, based on 'shoulds', and there is an attachment to outcome that things need to happen a certain way. In Sally's case, she had the expectation that Paul would be excited to see her, enjoy the meal she had thoughtfully prepared for him, and be appreciative of this. She likely had some other expectation that because she had prepared the meal and cleaned their apartment, he would reciprocate this in some way. Perhaps through expression of gratitude, acting a certain way, doing the dishes, or doing her a favour. She took it personally that he fell asleep, although this was a plan that was entirely created by her, with no consultation with Paul whatsoever. In other words, she was upset when her expectations for the evening did not match reality. Although it was her plan and no one else's, others were expected to follow through how she wanted them to.

EXPECTATIONS AND RESENTMENT

Anytime someone carries high standards for themselves and others, they are planting the seeds for future resentments when things do not work out as they were meant to. Expectations impact how people think, feel, and behave. Expectations impact thoughts and influence interpretation and perception of events. For example, Sally interpreted Paul's behaviour adversely, perceiving he must not care. There was no evidence of this. All that is known is that he was tired. Feelings of anger, disappointment, and resentment are created by having expectations of how others should behave and ignoring reality.

These feelings, in turn, impact behaviour. Someone may lash out in anger, give the silent treatment, or make a mountain out of a molehill. In relationships, one's evaluation of another person can reflect expectations about that person, plus the value or importance they place on that person. People typically have more expectations with family, close friends, and intimate partners than with acquaintances, as they place greater value and importance on these relationships and expect more from them, as they are investing more in them.

> Feelings of anger, disappointment, and resentment are created by having expectations of how others should behave and ignoring reality.

ADDICTION AND EXPECTATIONS

With Addiction involving relationships, having expectations for how others should behave causes unnecessary pain and suffering and is fueled by control, fear, and shame. As in all relationships, there is powerlessness over others. No one can control how others feel, think, or react. *Hoping* for a desired outcome is one thing, trying to force it is another. Hopes are fluid and allow people to go with the flow; expectations lock people into going a certain way. Therefore, it is important to reframe expectations as hopes and goals that are less rigid, not attached to a specific outcome, and unfold as they need to. Life and relationships have a way of giving what is needed, not necessarily what one thinks they need.

Addiction drives expectations of others, as well as self. No one is harder on the self than the self. A characteristic of Addiction can be to strive for perfection, which means having high standards and unrealistic expectations. In other words, to be something that is not real. People may live their lives based on what their parents, spouse, friends, coworkers, sponsor, media, and/or society think is best. People ignore their inner voice and do not speak their truth. They are so busy pleasing everybody, living up to other people's expectations, that they lose a sense of who they are, what makes them happy, and what they value and need. A goal of recovery is learning to let go of the disease and others' expectations and start living life based on one's own needs and values.

With Addiction involving relationships, people may find themselves in a relationship that does not mirror what they 'expect', which can leave them feeling hurt or used. For example, they may expect to be treated with respect, which to them, means being asked for their opinion on things, yet that is not happening. Values, such as that of respect, are personally defined and need to be talked about in a relationship so that there is mutual understanding and appreciation of where the other person is coming from. For instance, the other person in this relationship may believe that respect means taking the lead on certain decisions. These personal values are not something one can expect or impose on others. With expectations, beliefs and values are put onto others, and there is expectation for them to play along, regardless of their values, thoughts, and feelings. Expectations are created internally, infused with judgment based on "what I would do," and then projected onto others.

Expectations are like writing a screenplay for someone and berating them for not playing the intended role, even though they have not seen the script. It is not surprising that life and relationships are not in alignment with expectations, as these are rigid, judgmental, closed-minded, and lack reality. What is needed is to throw out the script, accept reality as it is (without judgment), and have the courage to act in accordance with one's own needs and values, rather than preconceived ideas or expectations.

> Expectations are like writing a screenplay for someone and berating them for not playing the intended role, even though they have not seen the script.

Chapter 6: Control

"I grew up in a household that was quite out of control. I was raised by a single mom who had support from her parents, but finances were tight and we often struggled to make ends meet, including rent and putting food on the table. I started working when I was young, so that I could contribute. Before that, I would monitor the food and money available, doing what I could to make sure there was enough for my mom and I. She wasn't very healthy, so I also monitored her health and sometimes had to call my grandparents or 911 if she was really struggling. As I grew older, I found it most comfortable when I was in charge. I am a great planner, and I was comfortable taking control of money. When I met my current partner, he was a good money manager, but it took me many years to feel comfortable involving him in the process. I preferred doing the planning for events, finances, and basically everything. I have rituals before going to bed or leaving the home to make sure every-thing is safe – lights and stove are off, doors properly locked, etc. When things are uncertain, I become extremely stressed, anxious, and fearful. Being out of control, or helpless, is the most uncom-fortable feeling for me."

    —Jerad

The illusion of control – over people, events, or circumstances – is one of the most convincing thought distortions the brain can play. The idea that one has the power to influence people, systems, situations, or feelings in any significant way is quite preposterous, yet the brain convinces us that this control is possible. Look at the precarious and complex nature of the systems and world around; the sequence of events that lead to a thought, feeling, idea, or outcome; these are so beyond one's comprehension and ability to plan or organize that it forces us to really look at the truth when it comes to (the illusion of) control.

CONTROL VS. ACTION

Sometimes one needs to act. This action can have an impact on situations and people. This idea is built into *The Serenity Prayer*, which talks about having the courage to act on the things that can be changed, but only after one has asked for the serenity to accept the things that cannot be changed. Control propels us to want to fix, manage, and control everything that is unsettling or distasteful, rather than exploring what is out of our sphere of influence, which is most things. Just because an action has had an impact on others does not mean it has caused that reaction. People will react how they are programmed and vulnerable to react; the action merely acts as an opportunity for response.

Control is like looking through a straw – the vision is tiny, narrow, and focused on a particular outcome that is visible at the other end of the straw. This view is quite limiting, as there is a whole world beyond the narrow scope of the straw. There is an expectation for what will be at the other end and of how to get there. Control eliminates flexibility, spontaneity, and the ability to be in process and work with what is presented along the way. For example, in Jerad's life, there were likely many invitations for something different along the way, but he was so consumed looking through the straw to his version of security that he had no opportunity to see or engage with them.

The desire to control is rooted in fear and insecurity. There is no trust in others or self. The brain cannot trust in an outcome or process that was created by someone else. There is tremendous ego and grandiosity involved in this; that somehow an individual is powerful and wise enough to know what the best path is for self and others and how to get there. Sounds like fantastical thinking, which it is, but the illusion of control can be very enticing as it provides a solution to the fear and insecurity: comfort through predictability. There is safety when there is a plan and associated action. There is insecurity when there is not a plan and the future is a tabula rasa, or blank slate. Venturing into the unknown requires courage, strength, and faith.

> The desire to control is
> rooted in fear and insecurity.

There is no spirituality or faith when it comes to control, only rigid thinking, expectations, and narrow-mindedness. Control may seem to be an antidote to fear, but is this really the case? As an activity, think back to examples when you were convinced something had to go a certain way (e.g., a work project, school grades, a holiday). As you went through this event, how did you feel? How had your brain told you would you feel? Likely, there is a discrepancy between what your brain was saying needed to happen and how it would feel compared to what really happened and how it felt. Sometimes the two – expectations and reality – are in alignment, which is how enabling of control happens, as there is more seeming evidence to justify doing it again. This cannot always be the case, however, and eventually expectations clash with reality and feelings such as disappointment, resentment, hurt, frustration, anger, sadness, guilt, and shame are the result.

Chapter 7: Avoidance

Anthony loved it when he got the opportunity to hang out with his old high school friends, even though he wasn't close to all of them anymore. Since they had graduated a few years ago, the group got together less often, as some were working, others were in university, and some were unemployed. Typically, they would go hang out at Jim's house, as he was renting a place downtown with some roommates. His roommates didn't care if they partied or stayed over, which is what often ended up happening. Jim had always been in the same group of friends as Anthony, but they had never been super close. Anthony found Jim pretty controlling, and Jim always liked to be the centre of attention, especially around girls, which bugged Anthony. The last time they hung out, Jim was mocking Anthony in front of a bunch of people. Anthony's girlfriend had just broken up with him, and Jim seemed to find it funny. Anthony remembers being extremely angry, but he didn't want to make a big deal of the situation and didn't say anything. Instead, Anthony drank heavily. He doesn't remember much about that evening except that he was in a bad mood and avoided Jim the rest of the evening.

Anthony later vented to his best friend, Chris, about what happened with Jim. Chris encouraged him to speak up next time, saying he would feel better standing up to Jim. This caused Anthony lots of anxiety, as he didn't think he could say something to Jim.

The next time he was invited to a group gathering, he asked some friends to find out whether Jim would be there. When he found out that Jim would be there, Anthony ended up not responding to the group text and didn't go to the party. He was too embarrassed to talk to his friends in the group about what happened and ended up having very little to do with them.

Avoidance is a simple way of coping by not having to cope. It is a more subtle manifestation of control. It is a way to pretend that there is no discomfort. Being avoidant, rather than taking action, can feel like the easiest thing to do as it is the path of least resistance. It is common that when people are anxious about something, they avoid it, just as Anthony did.

The downside to this is that avoidance keeps people stuck. Feelings and stressors come up, and avoidance pushes them to the side. Instead of going away, these feelings and stressors sit and compile along with new feelings and stressors. Now, a person finds themselves with ten times the feelings and stressors they initially had, because there are ten stressors they have avoided. Eventually the dam breaks, and the feelings and stress floods the individual and can result in symptoms like feeling overwhelmed, cravings, substance or behaviour use, crying, rage, outbursts, self-harm, or suicidal or homicidal ideation. The original motivation, which was to avoid dealing with any uncertainty and feeling uncomfortable, backfires. The bottom line is that no one can work through anxiety, fear, and other feelings using avoidance.

> No one can work through
> anxiety, fear, and other feelings
> using avoidance.

BOUNDARIES VS. AVOIDANCE

A common question that comes up in recovery discussions is: What is the difference between boundaries and avoidance? To understand the difference, one must look at the underlying motivation. If it is avoidance, the underlying motivation is to ignore reality, including feelings (which likely include discomfort and fear). People-pleasing and image management are core drivers behind avoidance, as one does not want to take a stand that might create conflict (or perceived conflict) in a relationship. For example, Anthony was worried about sharing his discomfort with Jim. Connected to this may be fear of how that would impact Jim, others at the party, and people's perception of Anthony. For those who avoid conflict, they typically struggle with emotional discord and prefer objectivity when discussing differences. This keeps the conversation neutral and separate from the person, so image and feelings are seemingly protected. These conversations tend to occur when people are uncomfortable sharing feelings, as there is a lot of reality to feelings, and would rather keep things at a thinking or analytical level. This may also look like smoothing over discord whenever a difference arises, so that differences are never discussed. A person can do this by making noncommittal statements that sound like, but are not really, agreement (e.g., "I've heard a lot of people have that opinion"), and/or by using humour, jokes, and sarcasm to deflect from the real issues (e.g., "Wow, I shouldn't have brought that topic up! Haha!").

In avoidance, people find ways of not having to face uncomfortable feelings generated from people, situations, things, or activities. Those who are vulnerable to avoidance include people pleasers and peacekeepers. People who use avoidance to cope typically have a passive communication style, which has developed as a pattern to avoid expressing their opinions or feelings, protecting their rights, and identifying and meeting their needs. As a result, passive individuals do not respond overtly to hurtful or anger-inducing situations. Instead, they allow grievances and annoyances to mount, usually unaware of the build-up. Once they have reached their high tolerance threshold for unacceptable behaviour, they are prone to explosive outbursts, which are usually out of proportion to the triggering incident. After the outburst, however, they may feel shame, guilt, and confusion, so they return to being passive.

Avoidance keeps people stuck.

Avoidance can also take the form of silent treatment. This is different than a healthy boundary, though it may look the same in action. Avoidance is when a person is not engaging in a behaviour that they need to. Boundaries are when there is disengagement from someone or something that is unhealthy. In Anthony's case, he lost connection with a whole group of friends due to his inability and unwillingness to address his feelings and issue with Jim. This is avoidance. It is a different situation if Anthony decided, through reflection and processing with others, that connection with Jim is not healthy for him, that no conversation would be healthy or worthwhile based on past evidence, and, as a result, decided to establish a no-contact boundary for himself. While this may look the same in action, in that there is no contact between Anthony and Jim, in the latter case, Anthony would be acknowledging and dealing with his feelings elsewhere and would be mindful to minimize exposure to Jim but would continue having a relationship with the other group members, if he decided that was appropriate and healthy for him.

Avoidance is controlling, which can be difficult for people to see. It can be easier to see someone who is overtly controlling to avoid a certain outcome, but avoidance can serve the same goal. In avoiding any contact with Jim, Anthony is avoiding a certain outcome (e.g., perceived conflict, impact to his image, upset).

Rumination when thoughts pertaining to a certain topic, person, or situation persistently and obsessively persevere is another form of avoidance. When a person engages in rumination (overthinking), there is distraction and usually a focus on solving the perceived problem, so they are trying to think their way out of uncomfortable emotions. A common example is ruminating to try to escape feelings of uncertainty and what is commonly known as 'analysis paralysis'. This often looks like examining a situation from multiple angles to develop conclusions, strategies, and plans that provide relief. There may not be any action taken with these plans, but there seems to be an intellectual understanding. In this, feelings are getting avoided as analysis and thinking have taken over.

> Avoidance is about control.

The antidotes to avoidance are honesty, faith, communication, and being connected to and open about feelings and thoughts – all of which are further explored in the 'Recovery' section.

Chapter 8: Manipulation

Manipulation is a way to force an outcome, to get others to do what they think is best without considering them. In relationships, there is often an element of fantasy where there are expectations connected with how the relationship should be rather than how it is. One can start to feel that others in a close relationship reflect them. If those others start to do something that one does not agree with, compulsion may come into play to control or manipulate. One wants to manipulate the situation to get people on the 'right' track with how things should be. This brings the relationship back in accordance with the person who thinks they are in authority.

> Manipulation in relationships
> can follow a similar trajectory
> to the cycle of abuse.

The manipulator's position in the relationship is perceived to be undermined if things happen or choices are made that are different than what they expect; hence, manipulation is tied to expectations. Manipulation is a way of pretending to look after another's interests while trying to further one's own agenda, which may be misguided and misinformed. It is a covert form of control.

Sam was really upset and confused. He could not understand why everyone was mad at him. He had tried to keep everyone happy, but no one seemed to care about how he had thought out every-thing and what he had decided was best for everyone in the family. His daughter, Ariel, was only 19 years old and her boyfriend, Pat, was only 20 years old. Both were in university and Ariel had a promising future ahead. Sam had not liked Pat initially because of his liberal politics and inability to focus on what career he wanted to pursue, but over the past year he had come to accept him. The more negative he was towards Pat, the more Ariel became alien-ated from Sam.

As her father, Sam had such high hopes for Ariel, and every-thing was on track for her to get her bachelor's degree and then apply for medical school. Even Pat was supportive of that. Sam had been trying to reconcile with Ariel and hoped that she would realize that she needed to focus on her studies and not on her airy boyfriend. The pregnancy is what drove Sam to consider taking more drastic action. He was glad that Ariel told him right away, so he could work on making her see what was right for her. She wanted to keep the baby, and Sam knew that it was important to be supportive of her decisions, but he had come up with a brilliant plan to get Pat out of Ariel's life, and he was certain that Ariel would then agree to have an abortion.

George, Sam's closest friend, had made all the arrangements with the escort and the private detective. George had assured him that no one would know what was happening. It was a quick sting operation: The escort would get Pat's sympathy while pretending to be a new student with problems at university, then get him in a compromising situation, where the private detective was on hand to take pictures that would convince Ariel that Pat was not to be trusted. He had not counted on Pat to have told Ariel everything about the sob story that the escort had told him, nor had he predicted that she would get involved in trying to help her, too.

When Sam tried to tell Ariel about his suspicions about Pat cheating on her and presented her with the pictures that the private detective had taken, Ariel was very quiet. He thought that she was hurt and needed time. She, on the other hand, did her own snooping and found out that the young woman in distress was really an escort. Ariel didn't know about Sam's involvement initially, but the escort identified George as the person who set everything up when Ariel confronted her, and Ariel was able to connect the dots as she knew George quite well and knew he was close friends with her dad. Now Ariel and Pat wanted nothing to do with Sam. Even his wife was mad at him, accusing him of being too controlling and over the top. Sam couldn't understand why everyone was so mad. Sure, he may have stepped over a line, but couldn't everyone see he was just doing this out of love?

SUBTLE MANIPULATION

Sam's story is rather overt, and this can be the case, but manipulation can happen more subtly, as well. When someone gives the 'silent treatment' because they do not like something that happens, the person affected by this can sometimes try harder to please that person. Hence, they are manipulated into the agenda of the other who is giving the 'silent treatment'. The initial desired outcome is more likely to happen out of appeasement and a desire to have a relationship. Many people think of manipulation as a short-cut to get others to do their bidding and follow their agenda without figuring out that it is someone else's agenda. It is a common pitfall amongst couples, family members, and friends where people go along to keep things smooth or the other person happy. Enmeshment with others increases the risk of manipulating others and getting manipulated when you least suspect it.

HOW IT FEELS TO BE MANIPULATED

If you are on the receiving end of manipulation, there will be feelings of doubt and insecurity as those who manipulate are incredibly skilled at convincing others they are in the wrong. There is a feeling of responsibility for the other person's emotions and happiness. Sam was blaming his family in his head (and likely out loud, as well) and putting responsibility for his feelings onto them. Often it sounds like, "I would be happy if only you would . . ." There can be a sense of obligation in the relationship, "I will do this if you do this . . ." yet often the person who is manipulating will not follow through on their responsibility and spin a tale about why it was not possible, reasonable, or fair for them to do so. Manipulation in relationships can follow a similar trajectory to the cycle of abuse, in that it often involves cycles of honeymoon, where everything is going well and riding an intoxicating high, to a build-up of expectation, which when not met generates tension, blaming, shaming, emotional and potentially physical or sexual abuse, to apologizing and promising of change, back to honeymoon. If there is identification with this cycle, exploring boundaries and detachment would be critical, as this is an extremely unhealthy place to be.

Another area where manipulation can happen is in the sexual realm, where sex is used as a promise, bargaining tool, or weapon. Sex is impacted by Addiction involving relationships in this and many other ways, as is explored in the next chapter.

Chapter 9: Sex and Lust

Sarah was happy in her marriage and had a busy life with her infant twin daughters. Sure, there was stress having two new babies, but overall, she was content with her decision to be a mother and to be married to John. Sex was more difficult at that point, as Sarah was having some physical pain from childbirth and was not feeling very confident about her body. She was carrying about 40 pounds of extra weight, despite having had her daughters six months ago.

Sarah and John's house was undergoing renovations as they felt the need for more space, light, and modern amenities now that they had kids. Sarah found herself watching one of the workers, Keith. He was different than the type of man she would normally be attracted to, and she didn't even think attraction to him was possible. She began chatting with Keith, offering him coffee and snacks when he was working by himself. Soon, she started fantasizing about Keith in daydreams and dreaming about him at night, too. Mostly, it was sexual fantasy and imagining herself doing things with Keith she had never done before in real life, even with John. Keith became the object of desire in her masturbation fantasy and she found herself acting out multiple times per day, whereas in the past, before kids, she masturbated maybe once every few months. Sarah thought it was healthy for her to re-explore her body and sexuality with herself, as she felt quite nervous and shy around John lately. It felt harmless to fantasize about Keith, as he was not her type.

Keith was happy in his marriage and life and appreciated the kindness offered by Sarah. He found himself watching her at times and was confused by his feelings of attraction towards her. He thought that she was attracted to him, too, but nothing was ever said. He found himself being more irritable and tense with his wife at home and preferred hanging out drinking at the local pub after work rather than facing his wife. It was wrong, based on how he was raised, to be attracted to someone other than his spouse, but fantasies of having sex with Sarah started swirling around in his head. Nothing ever happened with Sarah, but Keith found his fantasy became so strong that he sought relief with an escort, something he had not done in twenty years. The level of guilt and shame he felt about doing this outside of his marriage was immense. Drinking became an easy place for him to find relief from this.

LUST

Lust is desire. It can start innocently enough, with attraction to someone or something, but can take over one's thoughts and feelings in an uncontrollable way. Addiction is about attachment, so the brain has a vulnerability of becoming very strongly attached to ideas, images, or events and will perpetuate strong cravings until relief is found through acting out, which means engaging with the object of attachment. In the realm of sex and lust, this may be re-enacting images seen in pornography or other media; acting out with a specific person; or finding relief through sensation, such as orgasm. As is evident in the case of Sarah and Keith, engaging in fantasy feeds lust. It is like taking a sip of alcohol thinking that will stop one from wanting more. All it does is drive a stronger feeling for more because one sip will never be enough. People may say that lusting is all right so long as you do not act on it. However, the lust can become so powerful because of this engagement that people are more likely to act on the fantasy without full appreciation of the consequences.

Lust is a common symptom of Addiction and is directly related to fantasy. People can compromise themselves sexually, meaning entering a sexual relationship with someone that is not attractive to them because of what the person may represent. This was the case with Sarah, who was attracted to Keith for reasons other than physical attraction. Invariably, fantasy enters the picture and the affected individual loses track of their own reality and gets caught up in the fantasies that invariably lead to disappointment. Reality never lives up to fantasy. Lust and fantasy also have a strong connection to craving, which is a physiological phenomenon that can take over the thoughts, feelings, and behaviour of the person, such that they will act out even though they may consciously not want to. Afterwards, there are feelings of guilt, remorse, and shame for acting out in the behaviour, as it is never in alignment with the person's true self.

Reality never lives up to fantasy.

Although lust is generally attached to sex, by definition, let us also extend the conversation of lust into another area that is often called envy. In relationships where sex is not an issue, such as platonic friendships, lusting may look like wanting what the other person appears to have. This could be material things, such as money, clothes, or luxury items; or non-material prestige, power, or influence. This type of comparison is a common shame driver (remember that reality never lives up to fantasy). The person engaging in this fantasy and lust for more is left feeling inferior, inadequate, and less than. The experience may stay at this, or the brain may look for freedom from that discomfort through some form of acting out and/or trying to manipulate and control life to get the desired outcome, both of which are relief-seeking behaviours that fuel Addiction. A small douse of gasoline on the fire (the gasoline being acting out, including in fantasy, and the fire being Addiction) has an immediate consequence of some sort and keeps the fire burning, which creates long-term impact.

> Lust is directly related to fantasy.

Disease activity often starts with lust and fantasy, but over time, as tolerance builds, the brain may crave further stimulation. This can promote a transition from fantasy into behaviour, where now one finds themselves enacting the fantasy or finding relief through another behaviour that is tangentially related, such as Keith finding relief in sex with an escort when sex with Sarah was not available.

SEX AND TOLERANCE

Tolerance continues to build when the disease is engaged with, so people will continue to find themselves becoming frustrated and dissatisfied with behaviours that were previously intoxicating. This promotes movement along the sexual spectrum, and they may find themselves crossing lines they never would have thought possible, including things like sexual acting out with animals, minors, or other behaviours such as compulsive crossdressing, voyeurism, or frotteurism. These behaviours are often classified in the person's mind as being very different and separate from other symptoms of Addiction, which is not true. Tolerance and increased movement along the spectrum occur with all aspects of Addiction; this is a disease that looks for the highest levels of dopamine activity. As the brain gets used to a certain behaviour or substance, dopamine release is lessened so the brain pushes for something new, different, or slightly more extreme.

Addiction encourages pushing past one's own boundaries, values, and level of comfort, including in the sexual realm. One may find themselves in risky or dangerous situations that they would have never thought possible, which is possible and likely as the disease continues to be fed by sex and other behaviours or substances. One may also use sex for other ends, such as substances, like escorting to make money to purchase drugs or alcohol, or having sex to find validation, acceptance, or self-worth. Of course, this only fuels Addiction, which increases the likelihood that more relief will be needed to cover up greater amounts of pain, which keeps the vicious cycle of acting out going.

ADDICTION INVOLVING SEX

Addiction involving sex is a symptom of the disease that everyone with Addiction experiences. It is not a matter of determining if Addiction has impacted the realm of sex, but how. Learning how Addiction impacts sex for the individual is important for recovery from Addiction involving relationships, as sex is a part of romantic relationships. Learning how to have a healthy relationship with sex and learning how Addiction derails this helps one find balance, peace, and serenity. Sex can be part of intoxication, enmeshment, enabling, expectations, control, avoidance, manipulation, fantasy, stashes, shame, and sympathy on the disease side of things. On the recovery side, sex can tie into abstinence, withdrawal, boundaries, detachment, connection, staying in process, reality, honesty, faith, communication, and compassion. One needs to have awareness of how sex is influenced by Addiction in order to know how to healthily integrate sex into recovery. There are 12-Step programs that deal specifically with sex and relationship issues, including:

- Sexaholics Anonymous (SA)

- Sex Addicts Anonymous (SAA)

- Sex and Love Addicts Anonymous (SLAA)

If there are lots of questions or uncertainties coming up in this area, these are resources that may offer some clarity and support. Groups can be found in many communities. Information is readily available on the internet.

Unsatisfied desire creates a lot of frustration, while intermittent satisfaction or acting out on lust brings relief. Yet, it must be appreciated that lusting continues to feed unhealthy thoughts, feelings, and behaviours, especially in the context of Addiction, which is fueled by seeking reward, relief, or escape, taking one away from what is truly important in their life.

Lust and sex have a basis in fantasy, which was discussed in this chapter. In the next, fantasy beyond the realm of sex is explored as a symptom of Addiction involving relationships.

Addiction involving sex is
a symptom of the disease that everyone with
Addiction experiences.

Chapter 10: Fantasy

"I've been coming to the same coffee shop for the last year. Most mornings when I come in, Kelly is there making beverages. In my mind, Kelly is outdoorsy, has a large family, and a great sense of humour. I remember the first time I saw him – it was love at first sight. I knew he was the right person for me, inside and out. We have so much in common, as I also love the outdoors, family values, and a good laugh. Our relationship isn't perfect, but it's great. It's nice to have someone to spend time with. Getting engaged, married, having kids, and growing old together – I can't imagine doing it with anyone other than Kelly. I can also remember some of our bigger fights, like about where we would live, as we had different ideas about what neighbourhood we preferred and what type of house would best suit us and a growing family. I was also upset when Kelly didn't have any interest in hanging out with my friends, who are important to me. Some of these issues we still need to resolve. I find myself thinking about them often in my head, what I will say and how I can make the situations okay for both of us.

As I do every day, I take my tea, smile shyly at the barista, and leave the coffee shop. Maybe one day I will have the courage to talk to Kelly the barista . . . at least I think that is his name. I've never gotten close enough to see the name tag to know for sure. Until then, the relationship with Kelly continues in my mind."

—Logan

FANTASY AS A SYMPTOM

Fantasy is often one of the earliest symptoms of Addiction that people can identify, as the world of imagination is an option for escape, reward, and/or relief long before substances like drugs and alcohol enter the picture. Fantasy may coexist alongside other acting-out behaviours, like food or media, which may also be used from young ages for escape, reward, or relief.

What does it mean to live in fantasy? People automatically assume fantasy is living in a desirable imaginary place, but fantasy can also mean living in catastrophe and worst-case scenarios. Fantasy is living in a realm that is not real, often with scenarios that are highly improbable.

Logan's story is a great example of this. It is highly unlikely he will begin dating the barista that he thinks is named Kelly and marry him if they have never even had a conversation. In Logan's mind, he knows Kelly very well from some brief observation. In reality, he does not know him at all, and his brain has made up a story about who Kelly is, including his personality and interests. While it may feel appealing and rewarding for Logan to live in this fantasy, there is a lot of pain associated with it. Every time Logan sees this barista at the coffee shop, there is likely shame, sadness, and loneliness triggered, as he is reminded that he does not have a romantic relationship, has not had the courage to speak to the barista, and is unsure about the future of his romantic relationships.

Addiction thrives in this scenario as it creates the illusion of relief and escape when Logan is drawn into this fantasy world (it feels comfortable and soothing to be in it); meanwhile, there is a lot of pain and uncomfortable feelings activated that get covered up by living in the fantasy. Logan may not even be aware of these feelings, and hence, they stay buried. As they remain buried, they grow each time he sees the barista, as well as during other interactions he has in life that are related to similar feelings of shame, sadness, and loneliness.

For example, when Logan attends family events and is asked about his dating life, shame gets activated and he starts to run the familiar scripts in his brain of "What's wrong with me? Why don't I have a partner?" This is uncomfortable, so in the pursuit of relief, the fantasy of Kelly comes back in and soothes these feelings. It acts much like a Band-Aid covering an open wound, however. The fantasy does nothing to heal the underlying injury, merely covers it up so that it is easier to pretend the wound is not there.

> Fantasy is often one of the
> earliest symptoms of Addiction
> that people can identify.

THE PHYSIOLOGICAL IMPACT OF FANTASY

Acting out in fantasy provides a dopamine release. Even if the fantasy is rooted in painful imagination, it still takes one out of reality and provides a dopamine spike. Anything that is different or emotionally activating releases dopamine, which tells the brain it needs more of this and to remember to do this again. This builds over time and as Logan encounters new environments and situations where shame, sadness, and loneliness are triggered, his Addiction covers it up using fantasy, which stuffs the feelings further under cover where they continue to grow. This is another example of how Addiction operates as a self-perpetuating cycle. Sometimes fantasy is no longer sufficient to keep these feelings at bay, so the disease will turn to other acting-out behaviours, which may include anything from food to gambling, work to exercise, media to sex, drugs to alcohol, or it will 'up' the fantasy, moving along the tolerance-intoxication spectrum to something that does provide a dopamine release.

THE EMOTIONAL IMPACT OF FANTASY

There is the saying that 'ignorance is bliss' and many believe that those who are living in fantasy and disconnected from reality and their feelings are in a state of bliss devoid of suffering. This is not the case. People who are caught in fantasy are suffering greatly as there are moments where reality pokes through – no matter how strong the fantasy and delusion – and with it the crushing weight of the pain associated with avoided reality. Fantasy is turned to in greater quantities and extremes to avoid this building pain. While difficult to face, however, reality truly is preferable to fantasy.

The brain with Addiction will go to amazing lengths to protect its fuel and continue to find outlets to generate activity, which is where stashes can come into play.

Chapter 11: Stashes

"I entered recovery from drugs and alcohol in 2016. What this meant for me was that I was pursuing abstinence from all mood-altering substances that I had been using prior to that point. I recognized the substances were slowly killing me, and I wanted to live. However, it was difficult to maintain abstinence. I found myself picking up every few months. One time, I remember coming across some weed that was hidden in a toolbox in my workshop. I thought I had gotten rid of everything, but apparently not. I smoked it, as I was stressed out that day and needed a break, and didn't want to waste good weed.

Throughout my recovery, I would receive text messages from old girlfriends from time to time. Being in recovery and single, I figured it was harmless to engage with this, and I would hook up with them. The encounters were just about sex for me, I wasn't interested in a relationship, as I was really trying to focus on myself. I started seeing a girl more seriously in June 2017. She was a 'normie' and didn't understand much about Addiction, but she was supportive of me not drinking and drugging. Whenever we would argue, I found myself contacting some of these old sexual hookups, and we would get together and have sex. It felt good to be wanted and to not have to worry about reality for a few hours. The longest substance abstinence I've had to this point has been three months and two days, but I keep trying."

—Phil

A stash is a secret resource that is kept secure until needed. Stress, feelings, conflict, and craving may all be part of what drives the need to access the stash. Hanging on to substances that one is no longer using (or trying not to use) is the most obvious example of a stash. What could this look like? Keeping a store of unused prescription medication in the medicine cabinet ("It's old," "I never used it," "They were left over from a dental or medical procedure"). Having bottles of alcoholic beverages in the home bar or cabinet, even 'special' or 'sentimental' ones. There may be a convincing story that these would never be touched because they are too expensive, rare, or not to taste, but never underestimate how sneaky and conniving Addiction can be. In a moment of vulnerability, knowing that stash is there is what can make the difference between acting out and not acting out.

> A stash is a secret resource that
> is kept secure until needed.
> Stashes can be feelings, behaviours, substances,
> people, thoughts,
> and/or fantasies.

Stockpiles may be unknown, like in the case of Phil, who stumbled across a stash of marijuana. While keeping the marijuana was not necessarily intentional, the discovery of the substance was kept secret rather than reaching out to a support person and outing what he had found. This stash was not *necessarily* kept intentionally or consciously, though there may have been some intentional avoidance or minimization by the disease that may have been in Phil's peripheral awareness. Meaning, as he was cleaning out his house and workshop of substances prior to this event, there may have been an internal voice gently encouraging him not to be very thorough when checking the toolboxes, knowing this was where he would often keep substances in the past. So, while Phil did not consciously tell himself, "I am going to keep some of this for another time," the disease subtly influenced him to be avoidant, superficial in his search, and inadvertently hang on to that stash. The impact on the brain of the unintentional stashes will not be quite the same as the known stashes, but it will definitely be a vulnerable moment upon discovery of the stash and then, depending on where a person is in that moment, can generate disease activity for some time afterwards.

Never underestimate how sneaky and manipulative Addiction can be. It is very crafty about inputting thoughts, stories, and ideas into the head, and it is easy to be convinced that these are the self's ideas, rather than disease generated.

BEHAVIOURAL STASHES

Stashes beyond drugs and alcohol can be even sneakier, as they may be more subtle. What are some examples of stashes that are not drugs or alcohol? Relationship stashes, for one. Phil had several old girlfriends that he could contact 'on a rainy day' for escape, relief, and reward, which his disease was happy to do. In some of the relationship-based 12-Step fellowships, these types of stashes are referred to as 'rain cheques.' These are people that can be called upon later when stress, lust, and craving are high to act out with, either for sex, flirting, intrigue, enabling, or perceived emotional intimacy or soothing. These contacts are easily accessible and available. They may be former partners, friends there has been sex with, people of interest where no relationship or sex has been pursued, or anonymous contacts through various dating and matchmaking sites that are instantly available.

If there is vulnerability with online pornography and masturbation, then keeping passwords, browser histories, active online accounts, or apps on the phone/computer can be examples of stashes. The disease is leaving the door open for acting out, and it is content to wait. Even if there is high motivation not to engage with these behaviours now, they can easily be accessed down the road.

Even when behavioural acting out may not be a vulnerability, what about fantasy? This was discussed in previous sections and can also act as a stash. Those seemingly comfortable, secretive, private stories that the brain draws on to avoid and numb feelings and reality are stashes of their own. The fantasy is fuel that the disease can feed off of as needed. For each person, it is important to look at engagement with fantasy and how that is used by the brain. Sometimes it may be used as a stopgap when other behaviours are not available or may be satisfying enough on its own to fulfill whatever lust or craving is happening at that time.

A cell phone, in and of itself, is often directly related to Addiction. Whether this be through hours of escape on social media, playing games, reading news, browsing online, or more direct acting-out behaviours like dating apps and sites, pornography, ordering drugs, alcohol, food, or gambling. Many people find notification noises and alerts triggering as they provide a rush, which is the dopamine hit, often connected with getting validation, attention, or approval.

Those who are exploring Addiction involving food may find

they have stashes in their home, work, or educational environment. Foods that abstinence is being pursued with may remain in a cupboard, pantry, or tucked away in the basement where they may not be visible but are accessible. People who are around others, whether at home, work, or school, find it additionally challenging to navigate stashes. There may be foods where abstinence is being pursued (e.g., pasta), that others in the environment eat, so these foods are stored in the home and/or there is exposure to them in a work kitchen, when colleagues are eating, or around others at school. There may also be foods around that are continuing to be consumed that the brain rationalizes are okay to keep eating and/or have around. For instance, someone who has cut out sugar but continues to consume fruit juices or dried fruit and rationalizes this is 'natural sugar' yet is in higher quantities than they know is healthy for them. It is important to be honest about one's needs to establish boundaries and act in accordance with them. If people do not struggle with that substance or behaviour, then removing it will be a non-issue for them.

PAIN STASHES

Addiction fuels itself by storing away pain and later dumping this stockpile on the person, which feels overwhelming and drives a desire for escape and relief, which then leads to acting-out behaviour to find said escape and relief. These acting-out behaviours serve to keep the pain numbed and avoided, but it is not dealt with, which allows the cycle to continue: The pain builds, overwhelms, gets numbed again, continues to grow, and so on. In this regard, pain of many varieties can act as a stash – an amalgamation of experiences and feelings that have not been dealt with that are used to fuel the pursuit of escape, reward, and relief either now or down the road. The stash drives escape and relief from the pain and may also lead to acting out as reward for having 'gotten through' the pain.

What do pain stashes look like? They can be based on the critical, judgmental, harsh self-talk that consistently runs around in the subconscious brain. For example, "You are not going to be okay. You are a loser. How could you have done that? You are such a fuck up." It can be based on catastrophic thinking – envisioning worst case scenarios for life and loved ones. For example, that a job will be lost, resulting in bankruptcy and homelessness; or that children will die if they go away on vacation; or that a partner will leave upon discovery of one's true self.

Pain stashes can also be fueled by traumatic incidents from the past, including abuse, neglect, criticism, bullying, judgment, dysfunction, aggression, and any other exposures that the brain will not accept and let go of. Memories, dreams, and feelings keep resurfacing (often at inopportune times) and drive a compulsion for escape and relief from the pain. Even if people have done counselling specifically focused on reprocessing traumatic events, Addiction may continue to hang on to these memories, feelings, and pain and use it for fuel as needed.

There may be feelings of shame, which is also a huge pain stash used by the disease of Addiction. Feeling less than, unworthy, unlovable, and inherently flawed filters into self-talk and fuels catastrophic thinking. In shame, one feels incapable of dealing with any of these and unworthy of healing. The disease keeps people trapped by convincing them that

they deserve the internal pain and torment they are endur-
ing. So often people suffer in silence, thinking this is just their
lot in life. The brain gets a dopamine hit when intense pain,
including from feelings like shame, is experienced, as dopamine is linked to both pleasure and the experience of pain, as
well as memory and learning.

> Addiction fuels itself by
> storing away pain and later dumping this stockpile
> on the person.

THE IMPACT OF STASHES

The best way to identify stashes is to be aware of any secrets
that are being kept. These secrets may be around people, situations, thoughts, or feelings – basically, anything that one is
reluctant to share with others, especially others in recovery.
This is because the disease is trying to protect those secrets
(or stashes) and feeds the person stories that they need to
fear shame, abandonment, rejection, and/or judgment if they
share those secrets with others.

Listed above are some examples of stashes that one can
develop awareness around. As awareness builds, it is important
to act on removing these, as possible. There are stashes that
cannot be entirely removed as society is what it is – there are
liquor stores, head and/or cannabis shops, convenience stores,
strip clubs, adult sex stores, casinos, shopping malls, fast food
restaurants, cell phones, and grocery stores all around, not to
mention the messages received daily from media encouraging
certain looks, sizes, bank accounts, and external measures of

worth. There is constant exposure to people as well. The sight of an attractive person can spin cravings, disease activation, and fantasy, which can become a secret stash.

Some or all the examples in this chapter can be used as stashes by the disease of Addiction, which then get accessed if withdrawal or discomfort become too strong. No one has the power to remove all potential trigger sources. These types of perpetual stashes can be addressed using openness, honesty, and accountability in recovery. Communicating with self and others, any cravings, stories the disease is spinning, and feelings that are coming up helps support one in dealing with these ongoing vulnerabilities. Over time, the flashing, neon, billboard lights around these people, places, and things will become less overwhelming.

> Stashes act as a safety net for
> the disease – a soft place to fall
> if the going gets tough.

The impact of stashes is that they act as a safety net for the disease – a soft place to fall if the going gets tough. They keep the disease active and prevent withdrawal, as the brain knows it has something to fall back on when needed, particularly if it is not getting fueled in other ways. Stashes are a back-up plan for Addiction. If the brain is not receiving escape, reward, or relief through the ways it usually does, then these stashes can be utilized for that purpose. The stashes may be the same behaviour the brain prefers (e.g., stashes of drugs if the brain prefers drugs, food if it gravitates towards food), or different, with varying levels of associated activation. For example, one's stash is prescription medication but typical acting out is with sex and relationships. For that individual's brain, the dopamine response from prescription medication is less than from sex and relationships but is a good enough back-up plan if sex and relationships are not available. It really does not matter how potent the stashes are in and of themselves; the fact that the stash exists is very potent in keeping the disease active and preventing withdrawal, which will then fuel addictive thinking, feeling, and behaviour.

As mentioned already, shame is a common and powerful feeling when it comes to Addiction and is particularly impactful in Addiction involving relationships and will be explored in more detail in the next chapter.

Chapter 12: Shame

Samantha was having more and more difficulty facing her friends. She used to see them regularly, but in the past few months, Samantha stopped returning their calls and texts, as she didn't want them to see her. She wasn't sure why she was isolating and avoiding them, and she felt bad about this. When Samantha met with her psychologist, she vented about how much weight she had gained since her divorce six months ago. She talked about feeling fat and ugly and being worried her friends will judge her if they see her. She talked further about her ex-husband always making comments about her weight. He would be critical if she put on ten pounds, let alone fifty!

After talking more with her psychologist, it was recommended Samantha consider going to a support group for people who overeat. Samantha was horrified to hear this, as she didn't feel her problems were that bad. What if she saw someone she knew at the group? This all seemed terrible to Samantha, and she found herself isolating further in the next few months, including avoiding appointments with her psychologist, as she felt bad that she couldn't follow through on her recommendation. Samantha continued to eat more than usual, including more junk food, and found herself feeling worse about her body, which made her feel ashamed to go out in public. She started to dress differently to hide her body and avoided looking at herself in mirrors. She put less effort into self-care, stopped doing her hair or wearing make-up, and just tried to survive the day until she could come home to her safe cocoon.

Samantha was experiencing shame related to her weight gain. She was having difficulty seeing her friends because she wanted to avoid the shame that was triggered by spending time with them. She devalued herself, and her expectation was that others would harshly judge her because she was harshly judging herself.

> People, places, or situations
> – real or imagined – can all
> trigger a shame response.

WHAT IS SHAME?

A self-conscious emotion, shame informs us of an internal state of inadequacy, unworthiness, dishonour, regret, and disconnection. Another person or circumstance can trigger shame, but so can not meeting our own ideals or standards. Given that shame can lead us to feel as though the whole self is flawed, bad, or subject to exclusion, it motivates us to hide or do something to save face. So, it is no wonder that shame avoidance can lead to withdrawal, numbing, or escape as an attempt to mask its impact. Shame, unlike guilt, does not make a distinction between an action and the self. Therefore, with shame, 'bad' behaviour is not separate from a 'bad' self, as it is with guilt.

Although many people use guilt and shame interchangeably,

from a psychological perspective, they refer to different experiences. Guilt and shame can go hand in hand; the same action may give rise to feelings of both shame and guilt, but shame reflects how one feels about themselves. Guilt involves awareness that one's actions have impacted self or others. In other words, shame is a feeling about self, even though it may be connected with others, whereas guilt is about actions connected to self or others that one may regret.

THE SHAME RESPONSE

People, places, or situations – real or imagined – can all trigger a shame response. Someone may, for example, feel inferior with public speaking and believe that others will become aware of this, as though they are discovering a flaw of the true self. Not being a strong public speaker, in the voice of shame, becomes akin to not being a capable person. Shame will be felt when you anticipate being viewed as lacking or inadequate in intellect, appearance, or abilities.

As a defense against shame, people may attack others verbally to disown their own feelings of inferiority. In order to escape shame's self-diminishing effects, expressing contempt toward another person, or shaming them, re-locates one's own shame to the other. For example, a husband who felt judged and inadequate by his coworkers may then become verbally abusive towards his wife. When she feels vulnerable, self-conscious, and needs his approval, he feels more confident, projecting blame onto her for any failure on his part. Another defense against shame is avoiding the shame triggers, as Samantha was doing in the example at the beginning of the chapter. By avoiding her friends, the mirror, and her psychologist, Samantha could seemingly avoid her feelings of shame. Of course, this is not actually the case, as the feelings do not disappear because they are being avoided. In fact, they only grow bigger.

Regardless of the trigger, when shame is experienced, other emotions are felt too. These may include envy, anger, rage, fear and/or anxiety, sadness, hostility, judgment, depression, loneliness, or emptiness. As shame is a toxic emotion, it can result in self-attack, feeling overwhelmed, and can distort how one views self and others. No one is immune to feelings of shame, and as with all emotions and feelings, it is critical to become aware of triggers, typical reactions to shame, and how to then take healthy action that supports recovery.

HIDING SHAME

Grandiosity and/or pride are another face of shame. Trying to make oneself look bigger or better is often a cover for feeling inferior or less than others. Taking pride in something can also hide something that a person is neglecting in themselves. Being proud of others is a common example of deflecting one's own shame. For example, a parent can express pride in their child's achievements as a cover for their own shame for not having pursued something of value for themselves.

People-pleasing is another way of relieving shame by seeking approval. The shame of disapproval can be very strong, as well; a person can become trapped in doing for others at the expense of themselves. It is challenging to look at all aspects of shame in a person's life, especially when the disease of Addiction readily provides a way to avoid it by seeking relief, reward, or escape.

While shame feels very uncomfortable and is a feeling many want to escape from, it is helpful, as with all emotions. The utility of shame is that it provides information about the relationship with self. If shame is high, relationship with self is low. If shame is low, then relationship with self is stronger.

How we communicate about feelings with self and others is another important aspect of Addiction involving relationships. The unhealthy side of this is explored in the next chapter.

If shame is high, relationship
with self is low. If shame is
low, then relationship
with self is stronger.

Chapter 13: Dysfunctional Communication

Linda has been upset about her husband, Stan's, lazy approach to the household and parenting. She feels he ignores his responsibilities, the house is messy and dirty, and their children are often late for activities that he is supposed to take them to. This issue has come up again, and Linda is fed up.

"Ugh, there is so much mess in the kitchen, I can't even cook!" Linda vents. Stan is sitting in the next room on the couch, watching television.

"Mm . . ." he mumbles.

"I guess I'll just clean it up myself . . . Sigh." Linda begins slowly tidying the mess, watching Stan to see what he will do. He switches channels on the TV, apparently oblivious to her angst and frustration. She makes a point of making noise with the dishes and cupboards to get his attention.

"What's for dinner? I'm hungry," he finally asks.

By this time, the kitchen is partially clean, but Linda has not begun cooking, and she is fuming. "Why is it always my responsibility to cook, clean, and feed everyone? You're just sitting there on the couch doing nothing! Why don't you help me for once?" Her voice becomes raised as she can no longer hold in the frustration.

Stan stands up from the couch. "Me! Why don't I do anything? For Pete's sake, Linda, all I do is work my butt off for this family.

I put in 50 hours at work this week alone! I don't have time to do all this pesky stuff at home. You have nothing else to do, and it still doesn't get done! You are the lazy one, here, not me." Linda is furious, hurt, upset, and feels tears coming to her eyes. She sits down at the kitchen table and says nothing.

"Oh, so now I get the silent treatment, as usual. Figures. Typical night in the McMahon house, huh? I'm going out, I'll be back later." Stan grabs his jacket and heads out the door before Linda can respond. She sits on the floor, crying hysterically.

Does any of this dialogue sound familiar? This passive-aggressive dance of communication is common in many people's lives. While this may not be how one communicates all the time, it may be a default pattern of interaction that comes up automatically and instinctually, particularly when stressed, distracted, or vulnerable.

The roots of dysfunctional communication often begin in childhood. It is important to consider the messages you received about communication, both directly and indirectly, to gain awareness on how these messages have informed communication today. It is also important to become familiar with how Addiction can impact communication. The influence is often this: As much as one may want to be assertive, the disease of Addiction in the context of dysfunctional relationship patterns interferes with honest and open communication. Expecting others to understand often results in passive-aggressive interactions.

COMMUNICATION STYLES

Passive communication is when thoughts, feelings, needs, and/or wants are not shared with others. They may also not be shared with self and are hidden behind people-pleasing. For instance, Linda is not speaking up about how much of a burden she finds the household responsibilities until she is near burn-out and feeling extremely resentful. This is not going to result in open, assertive dialogue. Passive communicators strongly dislike conflict, which increases the vulnerability for people-pleasing and caretaking to keep the waters smooth. Passive communicators do not like the boat to be rocked and, even if there is a tidal wave below the surface, will continue doing whatever they can to keep the water on the surface steady. This often means that their own needs, health, and well-being are sacrificed.

Aggressive communicators also have difficulty express-ing thoughts, feelings, needs, and wants appropriately. They will often default to threats, aggression, ultimatums, and control in communication. Aggressive communicators are carrying a lot of feelings and hurt, too, but are scared to be vulnerable, open, and honest. Aggression and conflict feel more comfortable and are a way to hide from their inner reality. Often, aggressive communicators were raised in households where that style of communication was the mainstay, and so it feels familiar, even if they recognize it is not helpful or healthy.

> Passive communicators will continue doing whatever they can to hide their feelings. Aggressive communicators are also carrying a lot of feelings and hurt, too. Both types are scared to be open, honest, and vulnerable.

How does the silent treatment get classified when it comes to communication? Giving someone the silent treatment – purposefully going out of one's way to avoid contact while still making it known to the other there is upset – is a passive way of being aggressive. It is controlling and hostile in its own way, even if no words are being spoken. It is purposeful in its intent, which is to let another person know there is upset and is often about hurting the other person. This is different than having a boundary of no contact. With a no contact boundary, the intent is not to punish or 'communicate' with somebody without words, it is about honouring space and needs for recovery.

> Most people flip-flop between
> passive and aggressive communication; there are very
> few people out there who are
> purely passive or aggressive.

Most people flip-flop between passive and aggressive communication; there are very few people out there who are purely passive or aggressive. However, the default tends to fall more on one side than the other. For instance, someone may tend to be passive the majority of the time, but as they become increasingly frustrated and resentful of not having a voice, they will eventually explode, which often comes out as aggressive. On the other side, someone who tends to be more conflict-oriented will have times where they feel shame or fear and hide how they are feeling rather than explode, but it may then get directed to another person or situation, as the feelings are still there.

Revisiting the scenario at the beginning of the chapter,

which type of communicator is Linda – more passive or aggressive? What about Stan? Based on the information in this example, Linda demonstrated a more passive style of communication (sighing, hinting about feelings) with aggressive tendencies (directing anger at Stan). Stan demonstrated a more aggressive style of communication with passive tendencies. He immediately defaulted to anger (aggression), but then he avoided a conversation and fled the scene (passive).

Taking a break if conversations become heated can be a valuable resource for returning dialogue to a more constructive and assertive place. The key with taking a break, however, is that there is a return to the conversation at a later point in time. Ideally, this gets communicated before the break is taken. For instance, Stan might have said to Linda, "I'm feeling really upset by what is happening right now, and I am going out for some air to cool down. I will be back in half an hour, and I hope we can talk then." This is much different than leaving and, upon returning, pretending like nothing happened or going right back into conflict with more ammunition after time to think, which is not what taking a break is about.

THE DRAMA TRIANGLE

We can also look at communication styles in the context of the drama triangle, where people fall into the roles of victim, perpetrator, and/or rescuer. The victim is the one feeling harmed and is often in distress; the perpetrator is the antagonizer or 'bad guy'; and the rescuer is the hero or knight in shining armour. Throughout the example, Linda was in the role of victim and seemed to be antagonizing Stan to step into the role of rescuer, while projecting that he was the perpetrator or abuser. Yet, it appeared that Stan felt victimized, as well, by Linda not appreciating his need to rest after work. Those who have a default of passive communication are vulnerable to the roles of victim and rescuer as they have difficulty being assertive, standing up for themselves, and prioritizing their own needs. Those who are more aggressive in their communication are more vulnerable to be the perpetrator and seemingly contribute to or create harm against others. This process of dysfunctional communication is not necessarily conscious or intentional, but these are the dynamics that unfold through repetitive engagement with unhealthy communication.

NON-VERBAL COMMUNICATION

Another important element of communication is body language. This can be used to reinforce the dysfunctional roles of victim, perpetrator, or rescuer. For example, closed arms, glaring, muttering, turning away, raised fists, standing very close to someone, slamming objects, hanging the head, avoiding eye contact, grabbing someone, and forcing one's physical body on or around someone are all examples of how body language can reinforce messaging.

In this chapter we outlined the dysfunctional styles of communication – passive, aggressive, and passive-aggressive, and how these can look and be reinforced. Often, communication patterns stem from early childhood and attachment experiences and carry forward through life. There are many other ways in which unhealthy communication plays out, including through sympathy.

Chapter 14: Sympathy

Joe was having great difficulty concentrating on his work. He just found out his brother, John, and his wife had separated, and it was bringing back lots of painful memories of when his wife left him four years ago. John had called earlier in the day in distress, and Joe could tell he had been drinking. He knew John had similar issues with alcohol that he has struggled with on and off, although they had never talked about it. Joe wondered if John's alcohol use had anything to do with the breakup of his marriage. He knew for himself that he drank a lot more frequently after his wife left him, and it had taken a few years for that to change.

Joe was feeling sorry for John and wondering what he could do to make him feel better. He wished he had someone who would make him feel better during his divorce. Perhaps he could provide that to John and prevent him from going down the same path that he did. As the older brother, Joe had always felt somewhat responsible for John and felt like he needed to look after him now. Poor John. He decided to leave work early and go and hang out with his brother. John hadn't asked him to come over, but Joe was sure he would appreciate it. They could commiserate, and John would realize he wasn't alone.

Sympathy is typically defined as feelings of pity and sorrow for someone else's misfortune. When people share the feelings of others, the vulnerability is to take them on as their own and feel similar emotional pain as the other person. As in Joe's situation above, he was experiencing his own emotional pain that was triggered by his brother's shared experience. In sympathy, one can feel connected, but it is a trap where people get stuck in the problem without necessarily appreciating what the situation really is and/or how to deal with it effectively. For example, Joe and John may find themselves running down their partners, marriage, and relationships rather than looking at the reality of what was going on in the relationships and within themselves that had contributed to issues. The sympathy becomes an avoidance and relief-seeking mechanism.

THE DYSFUNCTION IN SYMPATHY

With sympathy, relationships become dysfunctional and unhealthy, which can be confusing, as there are lots of mixed messages in society that sympathy is important in helping people feel connected to one another in times of hardship. The 'in sympathy' cards that exist out there are representative of this. The line between sympathy and empathy is blurred. Sometimes these words are used synonymously, though they are very different experiences and impact health and recovery differently. Sympathy enables, empathy heals.

Anytime there is a situation when a person feels pity for the distress of someone else, they are pulled into sympathy. This experience means that a person is reacting to their own feelings about their own situation, but seemingly reacting to the other person's feelings and situations. The distinction between the self and the other person's experience and feelings become blurred. Implicit in the notion of pity is that the person does not deserve what happened to them. When others are unable to prevent, reverse, or overturn what happened, they may feel their own pain, anger, and/or resentment because of their powerlessness and/or past suffering. True support is now lost because there is a blockage. The person hoping to support is blocked by their feelings and past.

Sympathy is often confused with empathy. Sympathy is when you take on the feelings of another; empathy is the capacity to recognize and identify emotions that are being expressed by others and bear witness to them without taking them on. Empathy is the ability to understand how someone else is feeling, not necessarily feel those feelings oneself. Understanding does not have to equal acceptance.

ADDICTION AND SYMPATHY

With Addiction involving relationships, it is common for people to become enmeshed with others in sympathy. To help and show support, feelings of sympathy arise and can feel comfortable, which further fuels enmeshment. Sympathy fuels enmeshment because people have the illusion of support and care, but sympathy is about projection (putting one's own feelings onto others), control (e.g., "Do what I've done and you'll be better"), and commiseration (venting about problems and blaming others without taking accountability). None of these things are helpful or supportive. Sympathy is fuel for Addiction as it perpetuates strong feelings of pain, distress, shame, and anger. Remember that in the brain, any strong experience, including emotion, generates a dopamine response, which is enough to activate and fuel Addiction. This is the main way in which Addiction involving relationships operates without any external substance being necessary. The experiences alone are enough to create physiological reactions that the disease is looking for.

> Sympathy enables,
> empathy heals.

With sympathy, people have a difficult time detaching from the situation, as their own emotional pain has been triggered. People may find themselves quite consumed by the other's situation when, in fact, this is being used to distract from or seemingly make sense of one's own situation. Sympathy does not help provide clarity, however, as the emotional impact is too strong and distraction too great for actual awareness and healing to occur. With Addiction, it is common to become pre-occupied and consumed by others and lose sight of one's own needs and neglect self-care. Sympathy provides escape from one's own pain and suffering, while one can claim that he or she is being supportive to others in dealing with their pain and suffering, so this perpetuates the victim and rescuer position.

In this and the preceding chapters, the common symptoms and manifestations of Addiction involving relationships have been outlined. Take some time to sit and reflect on the material that has been read and start connecting it, either through reflection, writing, or discussion, to lived experience. It is important to cultivate awareness of what Addiction involving relationships has looked like in your life as you start taking steps towards healing and recovery.

The second section of the book is about the recovery process from Addiction involving relationships and what that can look like.

Part II:
The Recovery

Chapter 15: Holistic Recovery

"Hi, my name is Pauline, and I am a person in long-term recovery. I have been pursuing recovery from Addiction since May 2012. What this looks like for me is I have been abstinent from all mood-altering substances, including drugs, alcohol, nicotine, and caffeine. I continue to explore my issues with relationships. I realized back in 2015, after being in a relationship with a guy for 12 years, that he was another drug for me. I turned to him for comfort. If I had a bad day, he would make me feel better. Just having him there made me feel better. I felt like I was worth something, and his presence hid my shame. Deep down, I still didn't believe I was loveable or even likeable, so him being there reassured me that I was okay.

I discovered that he was involved in online pornography in 2014, and it took me over a year to gain the courage to leave. I spoke up, said that I didn't like it, but I didn't realize he was trapped in his own Addiction at the time. He couldn't stop. I kept talking it out with my recovery supports, and they encouraged me to be assertive. Eventually, what this looked like for me was ending the relationship.

Today, after years of talking, crying, journaling, and exploration, I believe I am worthy of respect and health. I can now see I don't deserve to be treated as less than, by others or by my disease. I found a place of my own and have been enjoying my life for the first time ever. I go to 12-Step meetings at least twice per week, and I have a great network of people I contact daily. Sometimes this is for support, but often it's just to check-in and share where I am at. My relationship with my Higher Power and spirituality grows all the time. I still fight with it sometimes, especially if I'm feeling down or my disease is active, but I know my Higher Power has my back and is there to support me. I love gardening, being outside in nature, journaling, and I am continuing to practice meditation and yoga, which are more difficult for me. Being with myself still takes attention and diligence. Today, I am a grateful person in recovery, which I couldn't always say, and I am happy to be here. Thanks for listening."

—Pauline's share at a 12-Step meeting

WHAT IS RECOVERY?

> Recovery needs to be a daily priority.

A lot of people, even those who have been in it for a time, wonder what is referred to by the word 'recovery'. This word is often used to describe recuperation and healing after an acute injury but can also be used to describe the life-long process of doing one's best to maintain health while living with a chronic ailment, including the disease of Addiction. Recovery in the context of Addiction is an ongoing process with no fixed end point, as to end recovery would allow the disease to take over. What this also means is that recovery needs to be a daily priority, recognizing that without integration of it into each day, the disease will take over. What one does for recovery each day may vary and will shift over time, but there needs to be acceptance that life must fit into recovery, not vice versa. This does not mean that recovery will take up every minute of the day, but the state of mind of being a person in recovery will be perpetual and the prioritization of recovery over life will happen. Many people in recovery will check-in with themselves at the beginning of the day to ask what their recovery priorities are for the day. Perhaps it involves a start- and end-of-day ritual with some additional activities throughout the day that promote health.

WHAT IS HOLISTIC RECOVERY?

Recovery needs to be holistic, meaning that it supports health along the key dimensions of body, feelings, relationships, and spirituality. This is referred to as the bio-psycho-social-spiritual model. All these aspects of health work together and support one another. If only one or two of these areas is being prioritized, then health will continue to suffer as the disease remains active in the other areas. For example, someone who focuses exclusively on their physical health through exercise and diet but continues to isolate, avoid feelings, and feel spiritually disconnected will be vulnerable to their disease acting out in these areas or others, which contributes to pain in the individual.

> Recovery supports health along the key dimensions of body, feelings, relationships, and spirituality.

The remaining chapters of this book introduce the key aspects of recovery from Addiction involving relationships, though these apply to any manifestation of the disease, including Addiction involving drugs or alcohol. It is important to remember that recovery involves routine, diversity, and structure using the bio-psycho-social-spiritual approach.

RECOVERY ROUTINE

Routine means that recovery must be built into each day. You may not do the same things each day, but there must be habit built around recovery action. For example, this may look like a routine of meditating for 20 minutes, twice per day; daily recovery reading; physical activity in nature three times per week; community or group therapy meetings four times per week; reaching out daily; and journaling daily. These are not the 'shoulds' or 'must-dos' for recovery but examples for a schedule that incorporates bio-psycho-social-spiritual health. The frequency and activities will vary depending on the time and the person. In this example, there is a predictable flow, and this helps orient the brain each day. It is important for the brain to know what it will be doing, how it will be looking after itself, and when this will occur.

RECOVERY DIVERSITY

Diversity means incorporating recovery actions that touch on each of the four realms of health: body, feelings, relationships, and spirit. If these are not touched on each day in some way, recovery balance will teeter unpredictably. For example, not processing feelings can result in emotional constipation and outbursts of anger, self-harm, or other behavioural acting out. Not exploring spirituality can lead to feelings of hopelessness, inadequacy, and purposelessness. Lack of physical self-care can leave you feeling run down and unmotivated to engage in other self-care activities.

Finally, it is important to have structure, to know when and how recovery will infuse each day. With the activities mentioned above, there is an additional commitment to meditating each morning upon waking, physical activity during the day, social connection and meetings in the evening, and journaling to process before winding down for bed. This structure provides responsibility and accountability. We will continue to explore other aspects of recovery from Addiction involving relationships, while emphasizing that life must fit into a recovery structure rather than trying to fit recovery into life.

In the next chapter, there is exploration of the role of abstinence (with and beyond substance) and how that fits into recovery for Addiction involving relationships.

Chapter 16: Abstinence

Mandy was tired of having relationships that seemed to only last around four months. She realized that her pattern was to be in relationships with men who were emotionally unavailable. She would become needy as the relationship progressed, and the relationships would always end with her feeling hurt and rejected because her partners would get mad and leave, usually in a dramatic and sudden way. Mandy had used alcohol and drugs in her past, and it scared her that she had cravings to use again after her last breakup. She started realizing that men were a drug for her, and the only way to get healthier was to abstain from being in a relationship for at least six months. For her, this meant no contact with any of her ex-boyfriends, no sex, and no online dating. She chose these because all these behaviours had become compulsive and she had no control over them. She knew from experience that abstinence from alcohol and drugs was the only way to get healthier, so she was hopeful this would be helpful with relationships, too.

Abstinence, as defined by ASAM (2013), is the intentional and consistent restraint from the pathological pursuit of reward and/or relief that involves the use of substances and other behaviours. These behaviours may involve, but are not limited to, gambling, spending, compulsive eating, compulsive exercise, and/or compulsive sexual behaviours.

With Addiction involving relationships, the relationship becomes the drug, and there is a persistent desire for 'more'. The 'more' may involve wanting more intimacy, sex, love, or connection in the desire to escape and numb uncomfortable feelings. It may involve seeking more approval, rescuing, enabling, distraction, avoidance, caretaking, or intoxication. When Addiction manifests in relationships, the person loses their sense of self as the focus shifts to the other person to feel whole and complete.

> With Addiction involving relationships, the relationship becomes the drug, and there is a persistent desire for 'more'.

ABSTINENCE IN THE REALM OF RELATIONSHIPS

Abstinence from relationships is needed when the disease becomes too active and the individual's life has become unmanageable. It is not as clear-cut as abstaining from substances, as relationships are needed for health. Abstinence needs to be individualized based on a person's bottom-line behaviours. Bottom-line behaviours include anything that triggers the disease. Establishing personal bottom-line behaviours is something that can be determined with the help of recovery supports through 12-Step meetings, as well as with professional supports and through personal awareness. It is typically recommended to abstain from these bottom-line behaviours for a minimum of 90 days, at which time it can be determined if longer abstinence is required. A longer time frame would be encouraged based on whether these activities continue to trigger disease activity when they are brought back into behaviour. The disease activity may include a return to rumination, fantasy, and/or compulsive sexual acting out. If the behaviour is brought back in and does not trigger the disease of 'more', then this behaviour can be engaged with until information is offered by experience that a change may be needed. This information is often emotional, as the emotions will tell us when things are working and healthy compared to when they are not.

With abstinence, this allows time for individuals to cultivate a relationship with themselves again. Maybe they never had a good sense of self, or maybe they did but it was a long time ago. This period of abstinence is a time to work on making recovery a priority and rebuilding one's foundation of health while re-establishing healthy boundaries that support recovery. This is what Mandy had committed to in the case example, as she had found this helpful when looking at Addiction involving substances.

Sometimes people decide to abstain from relationships with certain family members as they find the relationship unhealthy or toxic and it may fuel the desire to escape or numb. Common feelings that are elicited in unhealthy relationships include anger, sadness, shame, helplessness, and fear, which may lead to controlling behaviours to 'deal' with these feelings. The individual may find themselves going against their values, engaging in unhealthy behaviour, and not being assertive in order to keep the other person happy. Abstaining from family members can be particularly challenging and painful as there are lots of 'shoulds' and expectations in society to stay connected with family, even if it comes at an emotional cost. It is common for family members to overlook unhealthy or inappropriate behaviour in others, or put up with abuse that they would never accept from others outside their family. It can take tremendous courage to abstain from these relationships, and there may be backlash from other family members when there is disengagement.

When a relationship is toxic, it is in the red zone, which means that abstinence is required as any engagement with that person is triggering and disease activating. There can be no contact for now, which can be an indefinite period, such as days, weeks, or months. Abstinence needs to occur until one feels safe and comfortable to re-evaluate this person's role in their life. When deciding on when and if the period of abstinence ends, it's essential to determine if there is any evidence of change with the other person. If there is, then a healthier relationship may be possible. If there is no evidence of change in the other person, it is unlikely that the relationship can continue, but people may still feel they want to try and check it out, hoping that if they change enough, the relationship's impact will also change.

Once a relationship is deemed safe, it is important to take it slow before proceeding further. For example, start with a phone call or meet at a neutral location. During this time, it is important to check-in with feelings before, during, and after the interaction to get a sense if further abstinence is required or if there is readiness and willingness to pursue the relationship again.

> Abstinence allows time to cultivate
> a relationship with oneself.

SUPPORT

People in recovery can find tremendous support from others in recovery, especially those with understanding of Addiction involving relationships. Talking to trusted people for support and feedback is helpful, and in this context, the person can decide who and what relationships are healthy and which relationships require abstinence. Upon establishing boundaries in relationships, this will precipitate withdrawal, much like when one detoxifies from drugs, alcohol, or other substances. Addiction is Addiction, and the process, with whatever it unfolds, is similar and the themes common.

Chapter 17: Withdrawal

Withdrawal from relationships is often characterized by feeling sad, down, blue, and lonely; lack of motivation and energy; isolation; and feeling hopeless, purposeless, and aimless, in addition to physiological symptoms like appetite changes, sleep disturbance, restlessness, agitation, and frustration.

Withdrawal symptoms are a signal that intoxication has happened or has been happening. The human body and brain always aim to maintain balance or homeostasis by adjusting the neurochemicals and hormones in the body to cope with whatever is happening. Once the intoxication, whether it be chemical and/or behavioural, is waning or has ended, the balancing appears in the form of withdrawal symptoms until the body and brain can get to neutral or homeostasis again.

WHAT WITHDRAWAL FEELS LIKE

Withdrawal symptoms are generally the opposite of the chemical effects. For example, for a depressant drug such as alcohol, withdrawal symptoms can vary from agitation and shakes to delirium tremens and seizures; whereas, for a stimulant such as cocaine, withdrawal symptoms are mostly depression and exhaustion. In addition, feeling restless, irritable, and discontent are non-specific symptoms of withdrawal related to all aspects of Addiction beyond substances. Physical symptoms of appetite issues – feeling anorexic or bingeing on food, nausea, vomiting, headaches, anxiety, and/or sleep disturbances are all common signs of withdrawal. Anger is another symptom of withdrawal, which is often experienced as frustration – not getting what one wants and/or expectations not matching reality.

Following that line of reasoning that the withdrawal symptoms are generally the opposite of the chemical effects, with relationships the intoxication is often the ease of feelings, a sense of relief or high, and a sense of validation and purpose. Therefore, withdrawal from relationships is often characterized by feeling sad, down, blue, and lonely; lack of motivation and energy; isolation; and feeling hopeless, purposeless, and aimless, in addition to physiological symptoms like appetite changes, sleep disturbance, restlessness, agitation, and frustration. Many people are unaware that Addiction involving relationships is real and comes with similar withdrawal symptoms to chemicals and other behaviours, so often symptoms are personalized as "something is wrong with me" rather than "these are symptoms of the disease."

Amy and Ryan had a fantastic holiday in Mexico for a week by themselves. Their families helped by looking after their children, Jason and Crystal, while they were away. It all felt right, but within a few weeks of being back home, they started fighting. Ryan became suspicious of Amy and started asking lots of questions about where she was, who she was talking to, and why she was talking to men through work. Amy started to get headaches and stomach pains. She ended up at the hospital emergency room with anxiety and panic. For weeks, she was afraid that Ryan was going to leave her and was convinced that their relationship was over, as she could feel Ryan pulling away.

WHEN WITHDRAWAL OCCURS

Withdrawal symptoms are not just present when a relationship ends. They can start to appear as soon as the intoxication wanes and/or the fantasy aspects of the relationship lose their shine. The holiday Amy and Ryan went on created more fantasy about what their relationship could be, which was a marked contrast to what their life was like day to day.

Amy feeling physically unwell was even more upsetting to Ryan. She wasn't available sexually as much as she was when they initially started dating. He became more suspicious that she was cheating on him, as he noticed that she was trying to avoid spending time with him. He decided to end the relationship, especially since there were other women who wanted to be with him.

THE SEEKING CYCLE

Seeking relief from withdrawal symptoms is a common driver that keeps people caught in active Addiction. People with Addiction often seek and find others with Addiction that mutually feed their diseases. In this example, Ryan's withdrawal from the relationship with Amy was so uncomfortable that escape and fleeing seemed to be the only option. It is important to appreciate that withdrawal is a necessary part of the healing process. It is difficult to connect with recovery if intoxication is still happening.

HOW TO DEAL WITH WITHDRAWAL

Dealing with withdrawal requires recognition of what it is and appreciating that it is a physiological phenomenon that is not life-threatening, though it is extremely uncomfortable. Withdrawal is so powerful that it can drive people to suicide. Taking one's life needs to be recognized as the ultimate escape or seeking relief. Research and clinical experience have clearly demonstrated that healthy social supports mitigate withdrawal symptoms more than any other factors. Withdrawal in isolation will make the symptoms worse; withdrawal in the context of support will ease the symptoms.

Healthy social supports provide empathy, understanding, and guidance to stay in the process. Sympathy, on the other hand, may look like understanding, such as "I've gone through this myself...," but is heavy on commiseration and consolation and becomes about controlling away the feelings in the other, which will not help withdrawal, as this will prolong symptoms. Sympathy can become a trap of victimhood. It takes considerable awareness and processing of feelings to face and let go of the feelings of deprivation that prolong withdrawal symptoms and to embrace the freedom that comes with the release from the cycles of intoxication and withdrawal.

> Healthy social supports mitigate
> withdrawal symptoms more than
> any other factors.

Amy and Ryan, for example, have the potential to embrace being single, go through the emotional pain associated with relationship withdrawal, and discover the freedom in exploring their real needs and desires, rather than repeatedly seeking reward, relief, or escape in various relationships. This exploration may lead to an improved quality of relationship with each other, or it may highlight that exiting the relationship is best for both. There is not enough information at this point about each person and the relationship to decide; any decision will be reactionary rather than informed.

Empathy involves helping each person take responsibility for one's own well-being. Honest conversations about emotions such as shame, anger, and fear require maintaining a present moment awareness, and accountability, rather than consolation. It requires acting and working on acceptance of life on life's terms instead of wanting things to turn out a particular way. Punishment or retribution are not helpful, whereas speaking one's true voice brings reconciliation with reality. This does not mean agreement with or condoning what happened or did not happen, but rather accepting that the circumstances around whatever was or was not determined, what did or did not happen. Effectiveness in acceptance leads to decreasing of withdrawal symptoms.

Grief, a commonly recognized feeling connected with loss of a relationship, is a manifestation of withdrawal symptoms, which can relate to denial, anger, depression, bargaining, etc. It is well recognized that resolution of grief requires acceptance, which connects one with oneself and all the other things that life has to offer without the presence of the person one may have lost through separation and/or death. It is important to appreciate that a relationship that has not worked out as one had imagined or hoped is not a failure, rather it is a reminder of what was not meant to be and an opportunity to connect with what was real vs. what was fantasy. Trying to make something work when there are some fundamental problems, especially when there are complications related to Addiction, can be a real trap of enmeshment that keeps people entangled in cycles of intoxication and withdrawal, sometimes for a lifetime.

Repeated cycles of withdrawal and intoxication can lead to a lot of shame and hopelessness that can easily turn into helplessness and despair, leading to the ultimate escape of suicide. As much as a lot of people associate suicide with depression and anti-depressants, medication can sometimes be useful in curbing those persistent thoughts, but ultimately suicide can still happen in those who lose touch with opportunities to work through shame and withdrawal. Medications can suppress symptoms, to some degree, but do not correct the fundamental circuitry problems that led to the brain generating misinformation leading to the diminished recognition of problems and the dysfunctional emotional response. Sometimes the anti-depressants can create a feeling of uncaring such that suicide appears to be the only option for escape for someone caught in repeated cycles of intoxication and withdrawal.

Without withdrawal, there cannot be recovery.

While the discussion of withdrawal highlights the pain and difficulty of the process, as well as risks, it is important to note the benefits of withdrawal. These may seem less apparent, but the benefit of withdrawal to recovery is essential, because without withdrawal, there cannot be recovery. Withdrawal is an indicator that the disease's pull and impact is waning and, therefore, creating space for health, self, and recovery. This benefit, while significant, may seem elusive and unimportant when in the throes of withdrawal. Therefore, surrounding one's self with people in recovery is essential, as it can provide this reminder of what one is going through and for what benefit. Another important aspect of recovery, which can occur before, during, and after withdrawal has happened, is boundaries.

> There is no need to go
> through this alone.

Chapter 18: Boundaries

Fred was getting sick and tired of Jeff not following through on his commitments. They had been best friends since Grade 1, and for as long as Fred could remember, Jeff would often ditch him when something better came along. Fred had never talked to Jeff about this, as he valued their relationship too much, but it left him feeling hurt and taken advantage of. Fred knew he needed to act, as his resentment towards Jeff was building and he was not okay with how he was being treated. Over the next few weeks, Fred started making plans with other friends instead of always relying on Jeff to hang out. He told Jeff about his plans and left it up to him whether he wanted to join in or not. Initially, he felt guilty about doing his own thing, but after a few weeks he realized he was having fun with his other friends and was okay with Jeff not being around all the time. A month later, Jeff asked Fred if he would go to camping with him. In the past, Fred would have said yes, no matter what, but now he felt differently. He told Jeff he would think about it and let him know. He needed time to figure out if he wanted to do this rather than focusing on keeping Jeff happy and trying to avoid losing the friendship.

All healthy relationships need boundaries. Boundaries are guidelines or limits that each person develops to determine what is reasonable, safe, and permissible for them. With regards to relationships, boundaries are developed internally to determine how we would like to be treated. This awareness can then inform how we respond when someone steps outside those limits. Simply put, boundaries can be defined as "what is okay or not okay for me" and "the line where I end and someone else begins." Healthy boundaries can include everything from speaking up (through words or action) when we feel disrespected, to advocating for self by taking self-care time.

> Boundaries are guidelines or limits that each person develops to determine what is reasonable, safe, and permissible for them.

AWARENESS

The first step in setting any boundary is self-awareness. Without knowing preferences or values, it becomes very difficult to create healthy boundaries. Once there is a clearer idea of preferences and needs, it is much easier to be proactive and create healthy boundaries. An integral part of self-awareness and boundaries is being able to recognize and acknowledge feelings. To set effective boundaries, there must be information about what works and does not work, which often comes through the level of feelings. So often people dismiss or minimize their feelings rather than listen to what their feelings are telling them. Being in tune with feelings is vital because by being able to check-in and recognize the feelings, this creates space from others (detachment). In the above example, Fred had not paid attention to his feelings for a long time, as he was more concerned with spending time with Jeff and focusing on Jeff's feelings and needs. Jeff seemed to be okay with the friendship as it was, whereas Fred was not. Only when he started paying attention to his feelings did Fred realize that he was feeling resentful, which allowed him to start making some boundaries, which included not automatically saying yes to an invitation. This is an example of a boundary.

A challenge for many people is weak or leaky boundaries in relationships. This leads to enmeshment; where a person is so encompassed by the other person's 'stuff' that they have no idea what is going on within themselves. By taking the time to be with self, reflect, and check-in, this creates detachment as there is recognition of self as a separate entity from the other. Enmeshment happens more commonly in long-term relationships and parent-child relationships, as there may be reluctance to create and implement boundaries for fear of hurting the other person and/or not living up to role expectations. This allows dysfunctional relationship patterns to persist.

TYPES OF BOUNDARIES

There are two kinds of boundaries: internal and external. Both are set by the person, for the person to optimize health and wellness. For example, an internal boundary may be not ruminating about another person (e.g., wondering what they are doing, thinking about, feeling). An external boundary is outward action. Fred acted on an external boundary by saying he would get back to Jeff after considering the invitation. This is external action that reinforces his internal boundaries, which is to be cautious and thoughtful about the relationship with Jeff.

There is no right or wrong when it comes to boundaries. The focus needs to be on what is healthy or unhealthy for each person, and this is learned through experience and exploration. Two common traps people fall into with boundaries are trying to get others to understand or respect their boundaries, which often means telling the other person what they are going to do and/or not do, and trying to get others to change rather than implement a boundary for themselves. An example of this would be Fred being upset with Jeff for not being respectful of the plans they have made together, and Fred telling Jeff that he needed to be more respectful and considerate. No one can control another's behaviour, so what Jeff does or does not do is not up to Fred, but how Fred responds is up to him.

Boundaries are about acting and changing behaviours within self rather than changing the behaviours of others. Boundaries do not have to be explained or clarified to others. The motivation to do this is often to get people's support and understanding for the boundary, which is also not necessary. Boundaries are set for the person, by the person, so other's opinion on the matter is irrelevant to action. In fact, focusing on how other people will react to the implementation of a boundary can halt action, as there is fear related to disapproval. If there seems to be a benefit to vocalizing the boundary, then do so. The potential benefit may be in practising speaking up and finding a voice rather than avoiding. The risk is that this desire to share is coming from a place of wanting the other person to understand and provide validation. If that is the case or there is uncertainty, stop. Do not proceed with vocalizing the boundary, put it into action instead. Leave the room, change the conversation, do not attend an event rather than acting with explanation. It is important to act for the self, even if it seems to upset others. Other people's feelings are theirs to sit and deal with.

HEALTHY BOUNDARIES

Relationships develop slowly. Signs of healthy boundaries in newer relationships include a gradual getting-to-know-you and building of intimacy, which likely will include multiple interactions and increasingly more open and frank conversations. Sharing one's deepest secrets at an initial meeting or a few meetings in with a social contact is an example of Addiction involving relationships railroading one's internal boundaries and is risky. The risk is there can be rejection, disapproval, disconnection, shame, guilt, fear, or enmeshment. This is true of sexual behaviour as well. Sex as part of a healthy relationship comes with time and emotional intimacy, which cannot be there in the early days of a relationship. Take things slow so that one can advocate for self, be true to one's values and beliefs, and recognize warning signs of dysfunction before being enmeshed in them.

In long-term relationships, boundaries will need to be regularly re-evaluated to see what is working and not. People and relationship dynamics change, so parameters that were once integral for health may become more fluid. A lot of assumptions get made in long-term relationships, as people believe they know the other and can predict thoughts, feelings, and reactions. This is not really true. Never underestimate people's capacity to surprise. Ask questions about the other's feelings, thoughts, beliefs, and values. Ask if there can be touch and intimate space rather than assuming that is okay.

In the longest-term relationship, which is relationship with self, boundaries are also integral. Boundaries will need to be established with Addiction. Getting to know and understand how Addiction prompts a person to think, feel, and react helps inform boundaries to be set, meaning, what thoughts get engaged with vs. not, what behaviours are entertained vs. not, and recognizing the disease as a separate entity within the self.

One's role with self is to:
• Be honest
• Take time
• Develop clarity on feelings and values
• Show respect and care
• Communicate openly with self and others

Once a boundary is established, people often have difficulty following through and maintaining consistency. For example, Fred's thoughtfulness around the invitation from Jeff sends the message that Jeff cannot dictate all the parameters of the relationship, but if Fred does not maintain this approach and defaults back to saying yes to anything Jeff offers, this will give a mixed message to the other. It is likely Jeff will continue with the same behaviour, and nothing will change in the relationship. Inconsistency can be especially difficult with children when sometimes they hear "no" and other times they hear "maybe" or "yes." For example, it has been established that a child cannot engage with screens/electronics after 8:00 p.m. For three days of the week, the parent maintains this boundary, but the child continues to push for their way, and after a long, busy day, the parent allows them to use their electronic device. This may be a one-off, but chances are that, before long, the unhealthy evening routine is back. The other person (in this case, the child) is often blamed for the lack of change and follow through when, in reality, it was the parent who was inconsistent, which impacts everyone.

Some boundaries become permanent, whereas others are fluid or dynamic. A permanent boundary may be always walking away from someone that is being verbally abusive. A fluid boundary may be not engaging with a friend in active Addiction. If there is evidence of change in the friend (e.g., they start to re-engage in recovery) and that a healthy relationship with them is possible, the boundaries shift. When they were in active disease, there may have been a no-contact boundary which included not responding to phone calls, texts, or e-mails. As there is evidence from seeing them in 12-Step meetings of change, this may open the possibility of re-engaging through text to see how that feels. If it is comfortable, then a phone call. If that feels comfortable, then a face-to-face meeting may happen. The boundaries can shift gradually and are based on feelings.

Checking in on feelings gives valuable information about what is working in relationships and what is not. When there is strong evidence and feeling that things are not working in a relationship, it may be necessary to detach from some or all of that relationship with love.

Chapter 19: Detachment with Love

"My daughter has struggled with this disease [of Addiction] for years. I tried everything to help her and nothing worked, she just got sicker and sicker. I finally realized the only thing that was left for me to do was help myself. I learned that I needed to detach, and this finally made sense to me after years of trying to control the problem. When I first heard the word 'detachment,' I thought it sounded mean and cold. How could I possibly not care about my daughter? I realize now it doesn't mean that I don't care. I care greatly, but I can't save someone who doesn't want to take care of herself and is too sick to see reality. Now I am working on detaching, with love, of course, as I care about my daughter deeply, while learning to have boundaries and look after myself. I am starting to look at my own issues with relationships, recognizing that the desperation I felt to help my daughter was no different than the desperation she feels for drugs. That was a scary thought. Now I feel empowered as I realize there is help and the opportunity to get healthier within myself."

—*Simon*

Addiction is all about dysfunctional attachment. Often this attachment becomes hurtful, as it may be related to substances, behaviours, or people that are not supportive of health. The brain with Addiction continues to crave these substances, behaviours, or people, nevertheless. Simon's brain craved the relief of his daughter getting help and being healthy, which fostered an unhealthy attachment in his brain to her and her thoughts, feelings, and behaviour. Simon spent more time living in his daughter's head than in his own. This is what is behind the encouragement for people to detach. Part of detachment involves boundaries (internal and external) and another part is severing the internal umbilical cord to whatever it is the brain has become attached to in a dysfunctional way.

People may have implemented boundaries that prevent further activation of the disease. For example, not having contact with an individual for some time, not responding to messages that are looking for rescue (e.g., money, rides, commiseration), or starting to act on bio-psycho-social-spiritual recovery for oneself. These actions are all helpful; however, there may still be attachment at the level of feeling and spirit to another person. This means that unhealthy attachment can still be present, even when there is physical disengagement. This is very common in Addiction involving relationships – a person may be gone from life, yet the internal connection persists, sometimes for years or indefinitely. This may involve frequent thoughts of the person (e.g., "I wonder what they are doing now . . ."); fantasies (e.g., "I wonder what it would be like if we ran into each other . . ."); memory engagement (e.g., "I remember when . . ."); being caught up in feelings of grief, loss, sadness, or hope that do not diminish over time; or attempting to call, see, or view them online to figure out what they are doing. All of these are examples of unhealthy attachment. The need to detach would be prudent.

Addiction is all about dysfunctional attachment.

WHAT IS DETACHMENT?

Detachment involves acceptance of reality. Looking honestly at what the relationship had to offer, including the pain and difficulty, and how it activated and aggravated the disease. It is only when there is recognition of this that detachment can help a person pull back from the fantasy and come into reality. Often this means taking physical time and space away from the other person for the fantasies to fade and reality to kick in before re-engagement with that person is possible.

For Simon to detach, he will need to accept that his daughter's disease is out of his control and that his trying to 'fix' the situation contributed to harm for both parties. He will also need to start to let go of the fantasy of what his daughter and their relationship 'should' look like and start working with what is real. This may involve taking some time with minimal or no contact with his daughter, recognizing that anytime he is with her he is vulnerable to getting hooked back into fantasy, which can lead to caretaking, rescuing, policing, and dysfunctional attachment. After a cooling off period, he will need to explore how he can engage with his daughter in ways that do not activate this vulnerability. Perhaps this will mean only meeting for brief engagements in public places or not engaging in conversations about her health and disease. Each person needs to explore the healthiest ways to be in reality and detach from fantasy for themselves.

What does it mean to let go of fantasy? It involves identifying the stories that the brain has been creating about how one wants things to look, including in relationships. There needs to be recognition that these stories are not real and exploration of what is really going on in the relationship. Ask questions such as: Who are you in this relationship? Who is the other person? What are your needs, and are they being met? Are you able to take care of yourself, including speaking up for your preferences, in the relationship? These are uncomfortable realities to look at but necessary in order to start moving away from fantasy and into today. Letting go of fantasy is a key part of detachment, which can be accomplished through exploration and action, including by using boundaries.

As boundaries are put into place, awareness is cultivated, and detachment happens. There will be feelings that come, such as sadness, grief, loss, hurt, resentment, anger, frustration, shame, and/or guilt. It is important to spend time sitting with these feelings and letting them come in order to let them go. You will notice that, over time, these feelings continue to be processed and the ability to detach with love (not hate, anger, or resentment) will occur.

Detachment with love means that the obsession, rumination, and compulsion around that person will diminish and what will remain is compassion and empathy with boundaries. There will be understanding that the past attachment was not healthy for either person. There is hope for the best in their ongoing journey, while recognizing that it is their journey. Love means hoping for the best for people while accepting that what happens in their lives *is* ultimately the best, even if that does not fit with one's internal stories of best-case scenario. For example, if a loved one struggles with the disease of Addiction in more severe ways than one would have hoped, this is not necessarily a bad thing, it just feels bad. Staying enmeshed and trying to control also feels bad. Hence, learning to deal with one's own feelings, while allowing the person with the disease to find their path, ultimately feels better for both. Empathy and compassion (love) mean recognizing the feelings in self and others and taking appropriate action for self, which may mean detaching physically if staying attached impacts either person in a detrimental way.

RELATIONSHIP WITH SELF

In detachment, one unplugs from the focus on the other and plugs into attachment with self. This means prioritizing one's own needs, boundaries, feelings, and self-care in order to be present and engaged in relationships without turning to them for purpose, meaning, and validation.

Detachment may feel cold, cruel, or unloving. It is the opposite. Detachment may look cold, as there may not be active connection, but it is real. It allows each person in the relationship to be real and honest with themselves and bring their healthiest self into the relationship. Reality is kind, loving, empathetic, and caring. Enmeshment is dishonest and manipulative, whereas detachment is respectful to the self and other.

Detachment with love does not always mean no contact. It may mean detaching from certain parts of a relationship, like certain conversational topics, hanging out in certain environments, or seeing the other when the brain is craving escape, reward, or relief. If there is panic or fear that detachment means no contact, this is valuable information that there is attachment, and remember, Addiction is about unhealthy attachment. The disease does not want to let go of its fuel sources, and relationships are a big one.

In a healthy relationship there is recognition of self,

others, and the shared space in between, as detachment helps us move from enmeshment to healthy connection.

> Detachment with love does not always mean no contact. It may mean detaching from certain parts of a relationship that are not healthy or helpful.

Chapter 20: Connection

"I love having a group of friends that meet me where I'm at. For the first time ever, I feel I have people around me whose love, support, and care are unconditional. They accept me for me, and I can be whoever and however I need to be at any given moment. I remember I was having a really bad day and wanted to reach out to my ex-partner. Instead, I texted my friend, Jody, and let her know that I was struggling. She called me right away, and we talked for close to an hour. I shared how I was feeling, the crazy thoughts I was having, and she shared her own experiences that were very similar to mine! We ended up laughing about where our brains take us. I hung up realizing that the thought of reaching out to my ex had diminished almost completely, and instead, I felt immense gratitude and love. I am now starting to realize and recognize what love, care, and true connection is. I am so grateful for this."
—Alice

Humans are relational beings. Yes, relationships can aggravate Addiction, but healthy relationships are an essential part of recovery and health. Many people are stumped by the idea of a 'healthy relationship.' What is it? What does it look like? Feel like? Sound like? This is no easy thing to define in one chapter, but we can highlight some quintessential features of healthy connection, with self, others, and Higher Power. Enmeshment or commiseration about how bad things are can feel good at times but is a dysfunctional connection. As in the brief story above, reaching out to someone we think will help is sometimes not the best for us. We need to truly evaluate who will take us back into the trap and who can help lead us to freedom.

ELEMENTS OF HEALTHY CONNECTION

First, healthy connection is unconditional. This means true acceptance. There are no expectations or desire on anyone's part to change, and there is love, respect, and care for how the person is at that moment. Support is about listening, processing, and providing feedback as needed without control, judgment, or disrespect. An example of conditional connection is, "I will love myself when I have lost 20 pounds." An example of unconditional connection is what Jody did with Alice in the case example: she listened without judgment or ridicule and shared her own experience. There was mutual sharing not with the intention to change the other or make them feel a certain way, but because that connection becomes part of each person's processing and recovery.

Second, healthy connection is interdependent (not enmeshed or disconnected). Interdependence is where there is clarity on self, other, and the shared space between. In interaction, the person is clear who they are; their preferences, needs, and wants; and there is the ability to speak up about this, rather than becoming fixated on what the other needs or is looking for. There is time for self and others in interdependent relationships. Living interdependently with Addiction means learning to understand and appreciate the disease for what it is, but recognize it is part of self, not all of self, nor does it define a person or their personality.

Addiction is a disease and generates a recognizable set of symptoms felt by the affected individual and signs that are recognizable by those that understand the disease.

Third, healthy connection is diverse. No one person can meet all needs so a diverse support network of different people, personalities, and perspectives coming from a common theme of openness and vulnerability is important. Having connections with those who are in recovery themselves is also recommended, as people who do not have Addiction and do not understand recovery may struggle to see the disease vulnerabilities and give accurate feedback. These connections with others may not be with the people one expected, including family or past friends. The disease of Addiction has a powerful magnetic force and will attract relationships that are recovery hostile; therefore, a person may find themselves with a network of people that do not support recovery. For a transition into recovery to happen, these connections may become less predominant or exit completely. In recovery, relationships and social networks will shift, which can bring up many feelings that are important to recognize and process.

Fourth, healthy connection is respectful. Unconditional support is part of respect, as it is about being accepted as we are. Respect also includes having our voice listened to, as well as having our needs considered and honoured. If someone says they are uncomfortable with a sexual act and the partner stops, that is respectful. If the partner tries to manipulate, convince, persuade, coerce, or force this act to still happen, that is disrespectful (and abusive). A person may find themselves being disrespected or being the perpetrator of disrespect. Sometimes the disease of Addiction puts up a barrier to listening to another and is so focused on achieving escape, reward, or relief that nothing else gets considered. Connecting to self-compassion and self-care is essential for building respect for self, which then translates into respect for others. Self-care means doing enjoyable activities for self, honouring limitations and boundaries, and paying attention to feelings. Taking action on these regularly helps build up a relationship with self and self-respect.

SEXUAL CONNECTION

Sexual intimacy is a way to express connection in an already connected relationship. Sex with no prior intimacy is going to create the illusion of connection, but it is just that, an illusion. It can also be a way to distract from the disconnection one is feeling internally. Ultimately, in order to feel connection with others, one must feel connection with self and Higher Power first. Without this, we can use others to cover up feelings, which perpetuates further disconnection. Healthy sex is respectful, caring, and reciprocal, meaning that both partners are sharing their needs and engaged in the process. Sexual connection requires vulnerability. Sexual connection also requires safety to establish an environment where both people can be vulnerable. Sexual and emotional intimacy require vulnerability; therefore, a brain that is fearful of being vulnerable will create all sorts of barriers and safeguards for 'protection' that end up creating harm. Being aware of these internal defenses and taking steps to move in a different direction, perhaps waiting for six months into a relationship to have sex if one normally is sexually active right away in a relationship, can help establish different patterns and support health.

THE IMPORTANCE OF SPIRITUAL CONNECTION

Connection to Higher Power and spirituality is another important component of connection. What this looks like for everyone is unique. Higher Power connection can come through meditation, prayer, religion, nature, people, community, animals, events, objects, memories, or other places. Connection to Higher Power begins with openness and time, as all connection does. Taking time to explore, reflect, experiment, and see what is a fit. Connection to a Higher Power can provide guidance, support, unconditional love, a sounding board, and a sense of belonging. Many people have resistance with regards to exploring a spiritual relationship. Some have baggage from the past and feelings, judgments, fear, and shame that has not been processed. This is important to recognize and explore in personal reflection and discussion with others. It would be recommended to prioritize connection with a Higher Power and spirituality along with other sources of connection, specifically with self and others, for recovery. This avenue of connection is one that many people forget about or become distracted from by focusing on actions and rituals exclusively. In doing so, one can lose connection to the process. There is more to life than just the self and the whims of the disease of Addiction, and it is important to have connection to that bigger picture.

> Healthy relationships are
> an essential part of recovery
> and health.

Chapter 21: Staying in Process

"After being in recovery for a few years, my dad got diagnosed with cancer. I've had a difficult and interesting relationship with my dad. When I was young, he was abusive, drank a lot, and enabled my siblings to bully and harass me. I carried a lot of anger and resentment towards him for this. As an adult, he has been more open, vulnerable, and accountable for how he was in younger years. At first, I wasn't sure how I felt about his cancer diagnosis. I was scared, but at the same time, my brain convinced me I didn't care. He moved through treatment, had some scares, and today is in relatively stable health. My disease tried to guilt me that I had to be close to him and forget about the past. If I didn't, then what kind of daughter was I? At times, I did the dutiful daughter thing and took him to appointments and ignored things that were said or done that were hurtful. At other times, I was able to step back and let him figure things out on his own while I took time for myself. A few times I acknowledged how I felt when hurtful things were said. Today, I see my dad but on my own terms. If I'm feeling triggered or drained, I give myself permission to take some time with no contact and to cancel plans with my dad, if needed. The threat of death, which we are all dealing with every day (whether we realize it or not), does not have to mean I compromise my values or integrity. I move through this process moment by moment, day by day."

—Alexa

It would be tempting for Alexa's brain to label what happened with her dad and cancer a bad thing. It certainly felt bad at times, especially when fear was high. However, this was a necessary experience that facilitated learning and growth for Alexa. Addiction is fueled by avoidance, so there may be temptation to escape the situations themselves, and certainly the feelings, because they are uncomfortable. Staying in process means dealing with reality while recognizing that everything happens for a reason. Remember that discomfort, often more than comfort, is a great teacher.

> Staying in process means dealing with reality while recognizing that everything happens for a reason.

Staying in process is supported by acceptance and surrender. On the opposing side are fighting and control. Addiction convinces people that they know what is best when no one is that powerful and what one thinks is best, may not be. In fact, there are so many additional possibilities at any given moment that are incomprehensible, that narrowing the perceived options down to one that is best is limiting and ill-informed.

REALITY CHECK

Acceptance is acknowledging what is. For Alexa, it was accepting that her dad was sick, as well as her feelings of love, care, resentment, disgust, hurt, and hatred towards her dad. These experiences are real and can co-exist at the same time, though they may seem contradictory. Surrender is acknowledging lack of control and taking the hands off the steering wheel. There was nothing that Alexa needed to do differently because her dad was diagnosed with cancer than what she had been doing before. Her main responsibility was to continue honouring her experience and feelings at that moment. If that meant no contact with her dad, then no contact it is. Is this selfish?

Many people will convince themselves that is the case, minimizing the impact that living in a dishonest relationship can have on self and other. Saying that honouring one's own boundaries is selfish means that engaging resentfully, hatefully, or begrudgingly with someone else is better. This does not seem like a better option. It is disrespectful to self and others to live in violation of one's feelings, needs, and boundaries. With acceptance and surrender comes humility, which is an appreciation and recognition of one's lack of power. This is, ironically, empowering. One can then operate within reality rather than fighting for control in the realm of fantasy. For example, if Alexa kept fighting for the fantasy of a good relationship with her dad, she would expose herself to interactions that were abusive, disrespectful, and demeaning. This creates shame for her as she is obviously not being a good enough daughter still as Dad is not being a good enough dad. This is the never-ending cycle of the fantasy chase.

In process, one can be realistic and adaptive in their hopes and goals. This involves regularly re-evaluating action in the context of feeling. The feelings provide information as to what is working and what is not. The disease will prompt people to over- or under-perform; recovery is aiming to find some balance and homeostasis. Alexa needed to adjust her recovery actions throughout the process of her dad's cancer treatment, as sometimes she needed more intense support to process feelings and cravings coming up. If a person is in process, they are not beating themselves up for needing to make these adjust-ments, they accept that is where they are at. Alexa may realize in the future that she needs to detach from her dad completely and establish a no-contact boundary for herself. This does not mean that supporting him during his cancer treatment was wrong or bad, it means that her awareness and/or needs have shifted. She can take action on what is real today instead of beating herself up with the 'woulda, coulda, shoulda'.

What will happen and where life and relationships will go is uncertain. As much as the brain may try to convince of certainties or predictability, ultimately, there is very little of these. If one moves through life and recovery dealing with what comes up in the best and healthiest way possible, there will be freedom from attachment to outcome. Of course, feel-ings and reactions will come with what does and does not happen, but there will be fewer expectations and, hence, fewer resentments and disappointments. A person might not be where they thought they would be, but they are where they need to be. This is part of living in reality.

> There will be freedom from
> attachment to outcome.

Chapter 22: Reality

Cameron was starting to understand Crystal better. She had been taking time to focus on self-care and did not fall into his emotional traps to spend time with him as often as she used to. He was starting to realize, through journaling and reflection, that he had been over-focused on his work, justifying and rationalizing that it was generating income that led to him and Crystal being able to afford a more lavish lifestyle, which included going on trips and eating out at nice restaurants. Crystal had started to say "no" to a lot of his invitations, which was annoying to Cameron. However, she had been assertive in saying her piece and left him to figure things out on his own, in his own time.

He had demanded that she help him understand why she was doing this. She, on the other hand, said that it was not her place to make him understand. Crystal had encouraged Cameron to seek help for himself, professionally and/or through a peer network, which Cameron decided to do as he was feeling he could only get so far and so much clarity by learning and trying to explore these relationship dynamics on his own. Through this additional support, Cameron became aware of his tendencies towards control through avoidance or shutting down conversations that would allow Crystal and others to express feelings and preferences.

He started to see he was playing a role in the issues in their relationship, whereas in the past, he had placed the blame on her for not going along with the unspoken agreement of their relationship, which was to leave things as is. At least, that's what Cameron had thought he wanted and thought worked, until he started to see Crystal being resentful and pulling away. As he moved towards more openness and awareness in himself, he started to see Crystal was hurting, and he was also hurting from past relationships. Cameron had developed some pretty strong defenses to protect himself from being hurt again, but these protections were what was driving Crystal away.

What is reality? It is a difficult question for anyone, as it is easy to fall into trying to figure out what is right or what is truth. It is important to appreciate that, fundamentally, reality is subjective. It is one's own perception of feelings, the world, and relationships. If the brain affected by the disease of Addiction gives misinformation, one must be willing to consider that reality may be being distorted. Addiction creates a filter through which reality flows, so the input received at the end has already gone through this filter. Sometimes the distortion is stronger than others. Hence, to appreciate reality, one needs to be able to focus on awareness of what is happening externally and internally, have awareness of the general tricks and traps of the filter, and share with others to process. This processing will bring up reality that is closer to one's own truth rather than trying to figure out the objective truth, which is much more likely to be distorted. Even if other people agree with one's version of reality, there still needs to be caution in appreciating whether this is a sympathetic reaction, which can trap one in victimhood, or an honest, empathetic reflection from others, which allows one to expand awareness.

As much as Cameron was having difficulties in understanding Crystal, he elected to stay in process with journaling and checking things out with other people who could reflect more honestly and clearly on what Crystal may be saying to him. People who are not emotionally enmeshed in the situation, even if they are struggling with their own issues, can provide a more valid reflection of reality. If a person is willing to consider these reflections and stay in process, gradually reality starts to become clearer. People often see things more clearly in someone else's situation which, if they can connect with similarities, allows reframing of their situation to happen. If a person finds they are reacting to another person's sharing or situation, likely there is some reality in their own life from that situation. For example, if Cameron was listening to someone who was venting about their partner not being happy or receptive to their suggestions, this provides Cameron information about what is going on in his own relationship and life more so than it is saying anything about the other person.

> People often see things more clearly
> in someone else's situation.

PROFESSIONAL SUPPORT

Professional support in the form of individual and group psychotherapy can also support greater awareness. Group psychotherapy acts as a microcosm of the world and participants will find themselves running into communication and interpersonal challenges that they encounter in their daily lives. The benefit of experiencing this in group psychotherapy is that this is a safe place to explore and practice new ways of communicating and responding, whereas in life it may be more difficult to do that. Individual psychotherapy provides less opportunity for this, though it does happen, but offers the ability to cultivate awareness of ingrained patterns and reactions and be provided new tools and strategies to try out in life. Through experience with observations and reflections, one can spot distortions rather quickly in others and, over time, oneself. Being accountable to others in trusting relationships that are based on empathy rather than sympathy allows one to stay in reality rather than being taken for a ride by the distortions generated in the brain by the disease of Addiction.

Another integral part of recovery for Addiction involving relationships is living honestly.

Chapter 23: Honesty

"I used to lie about anything and everything, without even knowing why. Once, a family member asked if I was happy, and I said 'yes,' even though I was miserable at the time. I had gotten so good at putting on the mask, I started to believe my own lies. When I came into recovery, I still found myself lying to try and tell people what they wanted to hear. 'Sure, I believe in a Higher Power. Sure, I like 12-Step meetings. I feel great.' All the while hoping I'm doing it right and that people will love and accept me. Then I realized this still wasn't real. I remember sharing at an AA meeting my distrust in Higher Power and my lack of clarity around spirituality. This was three years into sobriety. I felt so much shame and fear. After the meeting, a handful of people came up to me to talk about their own feelings and issues with spirituality. One of them had been in the program for six years. It was then that I started to appreciate the value of honesty. I used to take on too much at work. Again, thinking people would like me more if I said 'yes' to everything, but I found people were resentful because I could not get everything done or done well. My performance review reflected this. My lack of honesty was catching up with me. It is a daily practice to catch myself, as the lies still want to come automatically, but slowly and with practice, my insides are starting to match my outsides."

—Alice

The disease of Addiction, as it impacts the brain, prioritizes intoxication, escape, reward, and/or relief above all else. This leads to irritability and low tolerance at a feelings level, along with manipulation and deceit at the behavioural level. The disease will make one say and do anything that it needs to in order to get a hit. This is true of the disease in all behaviours and can be especially obvious in relationships as people find themselves doing anything to get sex, love, attention, validation, conflict, sympathy, pity, or whatever it is their disease is seeking.

Health involves honesty. This means being impeccable with one's word; meaning there is commitment to and follow-through with what is said. If a person does not want to attend an event, then say "no." If this seems impossible, saying, "I need some time to think about it," is an important step, and hopefully, during this period of consideration, they can gather the courage to decline the invitation. If one finds themselves in a situation where the disease has said "yes" to something that does not support recovery, it is never too late to back out, even if that feels rude or disrespectful. This might mean leaving a dinner engagement halfway through or changing the RSVP at the last minute. This can generate more shame than taking time initially to reflect and honour one's feelings, but it will still be less harmful than participating in something that is fundamentally dishonest to self. Doing something that is not healthy is the ultimate disrespect to self and others, as it creates a false reality and perpetuates fantasy. For example, going to a comedy show for someone that has been called a friend in the past but there is currently no connection with sets up the illusion of continued friendship, yet the feelings say otherwise. This is confusing for everyone and can lead to resentment, hurt, disappointment, anger, shame, and other feelings down the road and can fuel more dishonesty along the way as the lie needs to be propped up by more and more behaviours.

In relationships, it is important to be honest about one's feelings. If there is a feeling of violation, something upsetting, or things are going well, it is beneficial to speak up and share this with the other person. It gives them information about the relationship. If the feelings are shut down, invalidated, or criticized in any way by the other person, then this is information that this relationship is not a healthy, loving, or nurturing one. It is better to know this through the process of being honest than be dishonest and continue living in fantasy. It is also important to be honest about relationship needs.

The disease of Addiction makes individuals extremely vulnerable to taking on the perceived needs of others; in other words, being who one thinks others want them to be, as Alice described. It is of the utmost importance to take time and space to be with self to get to know the self, including needs, preferences, and values. This internal honesty then leads to external honesty and assertiveness and provides greater clarity on internal needs.

> In relationships, it is important to be honest about one's feelings and needs.

With honesty there is integrity, which is when a person starts to feel whole and unified. Congruency is another word that could be used to describe this unification process. It means that what is being said matches thinking, feeling, needs, and action. If there is discomfort with a sexual invitation, then say "no." There may be guilt that comes in this advocacy for self, as the disease consistently tries to propel back to people-pleasing, but at the end of the day, there will be a greater sense of confidence and empowerment as one acts with integrity.

Sometimes being honest with self can mean being silent, which makes honesty an internal process that does not always require verbalization. Sometimes honesty will come out in conversation with others, particularly if one is being honest about how they feel about a situation. It is important to share feelings without being attached to how people will react or the outcome of doing so. Honesty is a process; it is not a means to a predetermined or projected end. It is the process of getting to know self and looking after self. If 'honesty' is being used to garner a certain outcome, this is manipulation rather than honesty.

A classic societal example is when a woman asks her partner how a new outfit looks on her. Does the partner speak honestly or say what they are supposed to say? These are all opportunities to explore being honest. In this scenario, let us say that one is not a fan of the new outfit. The woman gets tears in her eyes and changes her clothing immediately. Has the other person caused these feelings in her? Is it bad to be honest? The answer to both questions is, no. As we practice assertiveness and honesty, sometimes it will come out more harshly than intended, but this is not a bad thing. It is part of the process of learning and gives both people a chance to learn and grow.

At the end of the day, no one lives with the consequences of dishonesty more than the person who is being dishonest.

Living honestly, with integrity and congruency, provides freedom to be ourselves and develop more authentic relationships with others. To venture out into the domain of honesty can bring up a lot of fear.

The antidote to fear is faith.

Chapter 24: Faith

Faith is the antidote to fear, which is a big part of Addiction involving relationships. Fear can manifest where it makes a person think that the relationship may be in jeopardy, that the true self will be discovered and rejected or abandoned, or insecure in the safety and security of the relationship. There may be other ways that fear manifests in relationships. Love requires trust and faith in the absence of fear. This is true for love of others as well as of self.

Faith requires trust in the process. Even if thoughts and feelings are clouded, with faith there is a willingness to consider that there may be other factors at play than one is aware of. Trusting in the process means accepting that the intellect does not have all the answers. The absence of faith can lead to anxiety as one can gets stuck in fear related to what may or may not happen in future. The absence of faith can also generate a lot of frenetic activity to control various factors to mitigate against fear, which serves to increase stress. This attempt to control to reduce fear increases fear, anger, resentments, shame, hopelessness, and, ultimately, helplessness, which can feed or re-activate the disease of Addiction in a vicious way, with compulsiveness and/or impulsiveness increasing to seek reward, relief, or escape.

Faith is invariably connected to the recognition of

powerlessness that one has over the disease of Addiction
and unmanageability in one's life that results from denying,
minimizing, justifying, rationalizing, or attempts to control
people, places, or things by avoidance or trying harder and
harder. In 12-Step language, faith is connected with Step 2,
where one starts to appreciate the need for willingness to consider that there may be a Higher Power greater than oneself,
whatever it may be, that can assist in the process of getting
better. Therein lie the seeds of faith: the recognition that the
brain may not be able to grasp the situation in all its elements
and ramifications, but a power greater than self can will guide
one in the process of dealing with life honestly. Let us explore
a case example related to faith:

*Brendan decided to check out a SLAA meeting to see how other
people in recovery were looking at faith and how they were able
to stay in the process with their feelings, even when the internal
pressure felt so overwhelming that avoidance or control by seeking
relief, reward, or escape appeared to be the better option. Brendan
still felt a lot of sadness and grief related to Candace not being in
his life anymore. They had decided to take a break for three months
to each deal with their issues, but she had hooked up with another
guy who had more money so could take care of her and rescue her
from her financial issues. Brendan was feeling very betrayed and
had trouble with trusting a Higher Power that would allow such
things to happen, especially when he had been so understanding
of Candace's needs for boundaries and had sought professional
help for himself. He had initially thought that the professionals
would help bring him and Candace back together, but that seemed
unlikely now. The professionals had clarified over time, in several*

appointments, that their job was to help Brendan look at what was real rather than trying to fix a relationship in a way that he wanted. Initially, Brendan was disappointed and frustrated by this. The professionals were encouraging him to connect with his own feelings about past relationships and his attachment to Candace to see what his real needs were vs. the fantasy of what Candace could or would provide for him.

Brendan had tried praying to a Higher Power to help get him and Candace back together, but it was going nowhere. The harder he had prayed, the worse he felt because he felt frustrated that his Higher Power was not listening to him. At the SLAA meeting, he heard people talking about connecting with a Higher Power to listen to what may be best for them rather than praying to make something happen. It was very confusing as he had heard in his family and church that one should pray for what one wants for the good of everyone. At the meeting, people appeared to be talking about developing faith that what was happening in the present moment was the way things were meant to be and to trust that things may or may not change, depending on a big picture that may not be clear now or become clearer anytime soon. This left Brendan confused, but as he started to practice praying to turn things over to his Higher Power rather than looking for outcomes, he began to feel more comfortable with accepting what was and that he and Candace were no longer together. He slowly began to trust that he would be okay, whereas in the past he didn't think he would be okay without her.

In professional environments, with peer support, or in supportive friendships, people can talk about feelings of fear in a trusting environment where others may have similar fears.

Together, people can become aware that fear is generated by having expectations that do not match reality. It has been said that fear is not real even in a dangerous situation because one can train to deal with danger, which decreases fear. Whereas trying to get rid of fear by control often generates more anxiety, as in the case of Brendan. The harder he prayed and felt that what was happening was terrible and unfair, the worse he felt. His prayers were to get a particular outcome rather than trusting his Higher Power. Dealing with danger requires us to become familiar with the known factors and how to deal with them, while being aware that unknown factors may pop up that need to be dealt with to our best ability. Dealing with danger also requires one to respect limitations and not take risks that we are not skilled enough to handle.

> Fear is generated by
> having expectations that
> do not match reality.

Trusting and having faith in a Higher Power gives a person connection that is truly supportive. This relationship provides awareness that sometimes we must wait for circumstances or situations to shift, which they invariably do, to bring us closer to the reality of what is best in the circumstances. Just because the brain says that a certain outcome, like Brendan being together with Candace, is best does not mean that it is. If a person does not have faith and trust in the process, there is control exerted to bring about the intellectually desired outcome with no openness to other options. Faith also provides assurance that we may or may not get what appears desirable at present, as recovery changes our awareness and appreciation of reality such that we may not end up wanting what we once wanted. For example, if Brendan's relationship with Candace had continued, it may have eventually ended anyways after a lot of pain and dysfunction. The fear of not getting what one wanted dissipates over time when a person realizes that the initial want may have been generated by the disease of Addiction rather than what is truly in their best interest.

Having faith means staying in the process and being open to information that does not just come from the brain, which is where Addiction resides. In order to stay in process, there must be open communication with self and others.

> Faith requires trust in the process.

Chapter 25: Communication

Terry was bullied as a child and found it difficult to stand up for himself. When he was young, he would run away and hide from the bullies as much as possible. As he got older, he found himself in uncomfortable, even hostile, situations, and his immediate reaction was to avoid and hide. Terry decided to see a therapist; he was in a relationship that he felt was abusive but found it impossible to speak up in. During the counselling process, he began to practice speaking up and was able to say to his partner, "I am hurt by what you are saying and am going to remove myself right now." Eventually, Terry ended that relationship as he realized there was no amount of healthy communication that was going to improve the abusiveness. Years later, he found a partner with whom he could be honest, open, and authentic. Terry found it very refreshing to be able to communicate his feelings and perspectives without feeling criticized, judged, or minimized. He now had a voice.

Individuals like Terry are not alone, as many people have difficulty speaking up, especially in the face of hostility or aggressiveness. A necessary ingredient to all relationships, including with self and spirituality, is communication. Through communication one can connect with and express core feelings, opinions, thoughts, and perspectives.

> For many, the inner voice has been quieted by the
> disease within. This impacts the external voice.

For many, the inner voice has been quieted by the disease
within. This impacts the external voice. How does one connect
with the inner voice? It involves paying attention to the feelings and the information coming from them. For example, a
burning in the pit of the stomach is a reminder that one is
not feeling confident, strong, or secure and is a physiological symptom that can indicate shame in the absence of other
medical conditions. This information allows one to then
explore the situation and context. If this consistently happens
with the same person, like for Terry with his partner, it might
be worth looking at taking a break from the relationship or
backing away completely, as there may be something about
that connection that blocks the inner voice.

Another example is a strong explosion of anger (which
is not healthy or productive communication) that indicates
hurt, pain, and that one's needs and boundaries have been
violated in some way. This explosion, even though the brain
may want to ignore it because it is shameful and painful, can
inform boundaries, action, as well as what one needs to say
(and not say) to the other and what one needs to process for
themselves. This internal processing can be done through
writing, art, conscious contact with a Higher Power, reflection, or talking and is focused on releasing the feelings, not
seeking validation, escape, numbing, or relief from them.

For external communication, it is important to use "I"
language in expressing feelings and thoughts. For instance,
sharing, "I feel hurt right now," would be an honest and

assertive statement as opposed to, "You are being such a jerk right now and are hurting me. You better stop." This becomes a threatening and controlling conversation as the focus is on the other. How much control does one person have over another? None. Therefore, saying things to produce a certain outcome, such as getting someone to behave differently, is an example of unhealthy communication as it robs the speaker of the opportunity to practice assertiveness and find true release rather than relief, which only prolongs the pain.

It is not always necessary to communicate feelings directly to the person where there is upset. This may be a novel concept for many readers, as many brains automatically default to control overtly or by avoidance, and many people believe they need to share what they are feeling with the other who upset them. This can easily become about controlling their behaviour so that they know what to do, and not to do, in future. Instead, when something happens or is said and one is experiencing feelings, it is worth taking time to internally process and share with neutral support people who are not involved in the situation how one is feeling, not why one is feeling that way. In processing these feelings, one may find that communicating to the person who was involved in the situation is not necessary and may, in fact, be hurtful or ill-motivated. If one is looking for apologies, change, retaliation, understanding, or sympathy of any kind, then do not proceed with a conversation. Take these thoughts and feelings to the journal instead where they can be released without attachment to these other motivations.

To have practice with healthy, assertive communication, it is important to have a network of people where there is some sense of safety and trust. Having assertive conversations can feel risky and vulnerable, so not having this support makes it difficult to practice. Finding support groups where one is challenged and has an opportunity to speak openly, whether during group or informal conversations before or afterwards, may be a helpful environment to provide practice that can then be taken into what feel like riskier relationships, like with friends, family, or work colleagues.

Communication with spiritual connections is also important. Relationships grow when there is open dialogue and communication. The dialogue with a Higher Power may look different, but messages and signs can come in several ways, including through intuition, feelings, other people's sharing, and a sense of connection. Be open in communication with spirituality; take opportunities to share thoughts, feelings, and perspectives rather than begging for support, outcomes, or tangible results. A Higher Power does not work in this way, and we need to find ways of communicating that opens us up to connect with the energy and spirit that is beyond.

Also take time to communicate with self. Relationships cannot grow or develop if someone does not take time to get to know the self before getting to know the other. Ask questions such as: "Do I like this? What do I enjoy? How do I feel? How comfortable was I around this person? How do I feel about myself?" This exploration can be through writing, reflection, talking, or a combination thereof and facilitates getting to know the person you are and what matters most, which can then inform external communication and action. A focus on telling other people what one thinks they want to hear, rather than being honest, is not conducive to building a healthy relationship, even if it feels good initially. Another way to build healthy connection with self and others is through empathy, rather than sympathy.

Chapter 26: Empathy

Emily just found out that her sister, Anita, is getting a divorce. Initially, she was shocked, as she hadn't seen it coming and couldn't imagine herself getting a divorce after being married for the past 30 years. Anita shared how angry and hurt she was feeling, how she wanted to get back at her ex-husband for how he had treated her. Even though Emily had no personal experience with divorce, she understood how Anita was feeling and wasn't surprised when one minute her sister was angry and the next minute she was crying. Emily appreciated that Anita would need to grieve the end of her marriage and would likely feel many different emotions in the next weeks and months. Emily and Anita had always been close and spent lots of time together, so Emily made sure this didn't change and she continued to be a source of support for her sister. Sometimes when they spent time together, Anita would do most of the talking, other times she didn't want to talk at all and made it clear that any conversation about her ex-husband was off limits. Emily respected Anita's wishes as she understood how challenging it was for her sister to transition to a new life and her role was to provide support and listen to Anita's experience as she was willing to share it. Emily also made sure to take time to process her own feelings of frustration, anger, disappointment, and fear with her friends.

Empathy is the capacity to recognize and identify emotions that are being expressed by others. Understanding the feelings of others does not have to equal acceptance and one does not have to feel these emotions themselves. Feeling the same emotions as someone else is sympathy. Showing empathy involves seeing things from another person's perspective so that we can understand and relate to their feelings, without necessarily feeling them. Sympathy and empathy can happen together, so it is important to separate out the sympathy, which can create enmeshment. Empathy requires some distance for emotional clarity. Characteristics of empathy include understanding, active listening, recognizing emotions in self and others, withholding judgment, and challenging one's own biases or prejudices.

Listening is one of the most effective ways to demonstrate empathy. With active listening, you are present and engaged in the conversation rather than being distracted, whether on the phone or thinking about something else. It is about paying attention and really understanding what the other person is saying. As you listen, pay attention to any emotional reaction coming up, as sometimes this can lead to sympathy, which is where one starts taking on someone else's feelings. An emotional reaction can be a chance to learn about the self if one is able to explore "What is coming up for me?" rather than getting lost in the reality of the other. Reflecting back the emotions that are coming up is sometimes helpful because it can provide mutual support and understanding, which can help both people better understand and clarify their emotions.

REMAIN NEUTRAL

Another important characteristic of empathy is withholding judgment and staying neutral. This is an important step when practicing empathy as people are often tempted to give advice to try and fix the problem, or 'make it right', and share what they would do in the situation. To be empathetic, it is important to gain a deeper understanding of someone else's perspective without immediately labeling it as bad or good. Challenging personal prejudices or biases is also important, which can commonly occur when interacting with different cultures that may do things differently than we are accustomed to. For example, a friend might share that her family has disowned her as she is getting a divorce and now has no family support. From a certain perspective, this may seem unacceptable, but to empathize, one needs to put judgment aside and focus on the other person's perspective. It would be important to explore how the person feels about being disowned. Who else do they know that this has happened to? What are their fears about the future? This would need to be done without blaming the family or figuring out ways to make them change or changing the friend's feelings about what is happening. In this, one would be able to get to a deeper level of understanding and gain a deeper perspective, which will help in cultivating empathy.

> Empathy requires some distance
> for emotional clarity.

Many people still struggle to empathize with those who have Addiction, even those with the disease themselves. People can be judgemental and are unable or unwilling to understand the person's perspective or situation, and feel they know best. The next time there is a snap judgment about another person, try to move away from this by:

A. Looking deeper at the person and learning more about them to see if this can cultivate understanding and empathy for the situation they are in;

B. Noting things in common with this person, because when there is appreciation of commonalities there is less vulnerability for judgment; and

C. Asking questions to learn more about them.

To foster empathy, it is important to continually challenge biases and assumptions. Explore personal beliefs and values to see if they make sense or are even real. For example, if there is judgment that poor people are lazy or that all people with mental health issues are dangerous, explore the evidence for this, where these messages come from (as often they have been assumed from others), and how these judgments impact self. A lot of assumptions and prejudices are bases on erroneous information that has become widespread. Education, openness, and listening can help shift from old patterns of thinking based on misinformation to a place that is more honest and real.

Ultimately, empathy towards others starts with empathy within self. It is important to listen, without judgment, to one's feelings and work towards viewing, feeling, and experiencing them from a place of freedom, without attachment or remaining stuck in misguided assumptions that may be projected on us from past associations, family, and/or society in general.

Empathy builds connection
with self and others.

Chapter 27: Compassion

"I used to hate myself and be filled with self-loathing. When I saw other people being sad or upset, I would get angry and feel like they were just being victims. I hated conversations with other people; group therapy was brutal at first, because all I heard was other people complaining and whining. How was that supposed to help me?

One day at a meeting the topic was 'compassion.' I had never given much thought to compassion before; it seemed kind of useless, to be honest. How would feeling sorry for other people fix me? Then one day I was listening to one woman's share at a community meeting, and for the first time, I felt compassion. Her story was my story and it cut through my judgment, criticism, and doubt to the core of love, kindness, and care. I felt for her, but more so, I was finally feeling for myself. Now when I listen to people sharing in groups, or even see people road raging, I wish the best for them. I was that person who was angry and fighting the world, but I now realize there is a different way to live. I have love and tenderness for others and, most importantly, for myself. I'm just a human doing the best that I can while I'm here. That's all I can do."

—Mick, four years in recovery

On the road to compassion, there is often a pit stop at judgment. Some people are at this pit stop for most of their life, whereas others recognize a way out. Judgment is all about the person judging, not about the person being judged. Ever heard the phrase, "One finger pointing out leaves, three pointing back at you?" Think about instances of past judgment. Has there not been a lot of that judgment turned at self? It is easy to get distracted and focused on judging others rather than looking at internal reality. Typically, people judge when they are seeing something in others that they see in themselves and do not like, or they are judging what they fear becoming. For example, Mick sharing that he saw others as victims was likely something Mick feared being. Perhaps he already knew he had a tendency to go into self-pity and victim mode, or he might have seen someone doing that in his life and swore he would never be like that.

As people continue down the road to compassion, they will encounter:

- Empathy – appreciating and understanding someone's experience without needing to take it on

- Unconditional love – accepting someone as they are

- Honesty – being open and truthful with personal feelings and experiences, and being able to hear those from others

- Faith – trusting in the journey that things are unfolding as they need to

- Openness – sharing authentically and being open to receiving that from others.

- As people start to open to relationships and experiences while witnessing them rather than judging them, there are times where the reality of what is being seen is too stark and clear to be ignored. For this reason, sometimes compassion involves boundaries and detaching with love. Sometimes the most loving and caring thing to do is step back, as to stay would further enable or hurt the other. For example, someone who is not open to recovery from their disease, who is acting out in a variety of ways, is not going to be best served by having their loved one stay close, watching and witnessing the devastation while getting pulled into it themselves. In the compassionate act of stepping back, partially or completely, depending on the need and circumstance, there is the potential for change because something is different. Staying and participating in the same pattern will produce a guaranteed result: sameness.

As people take these steps while being detached from the outcome and expectation of what will happen, it takes them to an interesting place. Compassion and care for others has grown, but along the way, so has compassion for self. There is connection to humanity and recognizing they are not alone in their experience, which promotes being aware, sharing feelings, and responding to self and others with understanding and empathy. Compassion is the ability to observe the suffering in others without getting attached to fixing it and/ or connecting with self-suffering that may arise as a result of that exposure.

> Compassion involves boundaries
> and detachment with love.

Self-compassion may be a by-product of cultivated compassion for others, or it may be the starting point. Wherever it appears in the mix, please do take time to be mindful, rest, enjoy life, and do not always take the easy road, but take the road that feels best for you. Ultimately, this will keep you on the road of compassion.

Chapter 28: Feelings

Two years ago:

"I have had trouble with worry and stress in the past but feel like that's kind of gone away in the past while. I wanted to talk to you today about my work, as it is something on my mind. I co-own and am supposed to co-run my business with my partner but often he takes over, and I feel left out and left behind. He has made some business decisions recently that I don't believe are smart or well thought out. I feel like these actions could bankrupt the company, and I have dreams of creditors, the bank, and the government coming after me. It wakes me up and keeps me up at night. Am I stressed? No, not really. Why do you ask?"

Today:

"I ended up talking with my business partner the other day and expressing all the feelings I've had bottled up for a long time – anger, fear, resentment, worry, stress, distrust, disgust, shame, guilt, anxiety, and judgment. I have so much more awareness today of what I am feeling. I don't really know what to do in terms of action sometimes, but I do know where I'm at often, which feels like a big step forward."

—Al

EMOTIONAL SOBRIETY

Emotional sobriety is the term that comes to mind as people open an exploration of feelings in the context of recovery. How many times do we see someone who talks about being sober or in recovery, yet seems miserable? They grumble about everything and do not seem to be coping with life. The difference between this person and another who is in recovery and has peace, serenity, joy, and the ability to laugh at life and the disease is emotional sobriety.

What is emotional sobriety? It is certainly not abstinence from feeling or pain. The spectrum of human emotion, from happiness to sadness to anger to shame to fear and everything around these feelings are a part of human experience and will be present as a person continues to live in recovery. Recovery is not the absence of feeling – that is the disease. This is the tricky addictive thinking, "If I can find a way to get rid of these uncomfortable feelings, then I will be okay, and my recovery will continue . . ." But is this not what Addiction is all about? Escape and relief from discomfort and promotion of reward? It is important to recognize when the disease is infiltrating recovery, and this is a common way in which it invades.

Therefore, emotional sobriety is learning to accept, sit with, and process any and all feelings that come up. We cannot pick and choose what feelings make it through the gate to be felt and those that get left behind. In the realm of feelings there are no good or bad feelings, there are just feelings. These feelings are a rich source of reality and information. One does not want to turn their back on this valuable resource because to do so means disconnection from reality.

> Recovery is not the absence of
> feeling – that is the disease.
> Emotional sobriety is learning to accept, sit with, and process any
> and all feelings that come up.

Relationships trigger a lot of feelings. If things are going well in connection with others, we may feel happy, content, satisfied, peaceful, agitated, fearful, worry, shame, and/or guilt. If things are not going well in a relationship, we may feel stress, grateful, hopeful, scared, shame, guilt, relief, sad, loss, motivated, detached, and/or ambivalent. Notice how the feelings cannot be labelled 'good' or 'bad', as they cover the spectrum. They are plentiful and will change frequently; hence, it is so important to check-in regularly on how one is feeling to learn what is going on inside.

Feelings inform action. For example, if Al had felt satisfied, equal, respected, valued, and content in the relationship with his business partner, then he likely would not have hesitated to speak up and voice his feelings. It is likely that there are other relationships where Al has a hard time sharing his feelings, as the disease of Addiction cuts a person off emotionally, and the awareness of his feelings can provide greater incentive to speak up and be assertive with others. The confidence in speaking up comes with practice over time.

> It is important to let the
> feelings come before you
> can let them go.

A relationship with feelings is a relationship like any other. It takes time to build up, so a first action step is to set aside five to ten minutes each day to sit quietly and ask how you are feeling. In a new relationship, there needs to be time set aside and effort put in to get to know the other. Once there starts to be familiarity with feelings, there will be times when more needs to be done than acknowledging their presence. There will need to be tools, such as writing, drawing, talking, and any other form of expression that is meaningful. It is important to let the feelings come before they can be let go.

Relationships can fuel a lot of feelings, and they can also be the place where we find unconditional support and a safe space for expression. There may be uncertainty as to how much can be shared with others; this will need to be slowly explored over time as there is practice getting vulnerable bit by bit, sharing a little bit more depth and feelings and seeing what the response is. Judgment, ridicule, disinterest, criticism, advice giving, minimization, dismissal, or hostility are signs that this may not be a person to go to, and there may be an inability to develop emotional intimacy with them. Openness, listening, realistic feedback, non-judgment, acceptance, respect, gratitude, honesty, and mutual sharing (meaning they get vulnerable, too) are signs that this is someone to explore developing emotional intimacy with.

The relationship with self will grow as feelings, awareness, and connection do. Feelings connect to intuition and inner voice, which is a powerful guide in relationships and life actions. The relationship with feelings opens up a powerful avenue of information and connection potential – with self, others, and spirituality.

Chapter 29: Action

Gaining awareness is part of the ongoing recovery journey but must be complemented by action. These work in synchronicity; one can promote the other. Sometimes by starting to act, awareness will come, and sometimes awareness will promote action. Through the reading, awareness has likely been coming. In this chapter are some direct questions and activities to clarify and promote action in ongoing recovery. We encourage taking time with these and using a separate tool (e.g., paper, journal, online document) for processing. Take care in the exploration and step back from the activities as needed. Some will resonate more than others. Remember, these questions and recommendations can always be revisited anytime.

QUESTIONS FOR FURTHER ACTION

- What chapters did you struggle with the most in this book? What feelings came up as you read them?

- What chapters were the most hopeful for you?

- What parts of recovery for Addiction involving relationships are you struggling with the most?

In the area(s) that you are struggling with (e.g., boundaries, communication, control), pick one small action that you can take in the next week. Build a commitment to this (e.g., tell someone, put it in your calendar, write it down). Later revisit: How did it feel to commit and follow through on this? What challenges came up in following through?

Challenge yourself to a daily feelings check-in. Sit quietly somewhere without distraction, take a few minutes to relax through focusing on breath, then ask yourself, "How am I feeling?" Take a few minutes to sit in this before moving on to any other action.

Looking at enmeshment, can you think of situations in your life when you went along with something only to realize later that you got caught in someone else's agenda? Write about the situation, then reflect and write or talk about:

- How did that feel?

- What did you do?

- What would you rather have done?

Looking at control, when have you manipulated or tried to force your own agenda or outcome on a situation?

- How did that feel?

- What did you do?

- What might you have done instead?

Looking at a reality check, write out some truths about a close relationship. If possible and safe, check these out with that person and with other(s) who do not have an emotional connection with that person. For example: That I am always the centre of the relationship; that I am always serious; that that person always has my back. Then reflect on:

- What did you discover?

- If you talked with the other person, what things were common between your perception of reality and theirs?

- What things were common between your perception of reality and the individual(s) who is not emotionally connected to your loved one?

- Are you able to identify feelings, expectations, or resentments that were clouding the reality of your relationship vs. fantasy of what could be, would be, or should be?

Looking at faith, explore:

- What has been your experience with faith?

- Have you had instances in the past where something felt like it was truly desirable but then the perspective changed as you became more aware of the reality of that situation?

- How did you cope with the process of not knowing what the truth was?

- Did you feel betrayed by your Higher Power?

- Were you able to connect with awareness that what may have happened may have felt bad but was not necessarily a bad thing?

Sometimes the most powerful action is to observe oneself, rather than doing something just for the sake of doing it. The process of being requires action that is mostly internal observation. Never underestimate the power of being.

We wish you the best in your ongoing journey of recovery and invite you to return to the concepts and various chapters in this book frequently throughout your journey, as what stood out to you right now will change as time progresses. Investing daily in action that supports your physical, emotional, relational, and spiritual health will help in dealing with other symptoms of Addiction that arise over time.

References

American Society of Addiction Medicine (Adoption Date: April 2011). Public Policy Statement: Definition of Addiction. www.asam.org

American Society of Addiction Medicine (Adoption Date: July 2013). Terminology Related to Addiction, Treatment, and Recovery. www.asam.org

Hajela, R., Newton, S., & Abbott, P. (2015) *Addiction is Addiction: Understanding the disease in oneself and others for a better quality of life*. FriesenPress: Victoria, BC.

Also available by the authors:

Addiction is Addiction:
Understanding the disease in oneself
and others for a better quality of life

Addiction is Addiction Workbook

Lightning Source UK Ltd.
Milton Keynes UK
UKHW011953220322
400453UK00004B/931